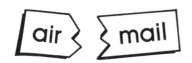

Compound Words

Some words are made from putting two different words together. The new word is called a compound word.

grape + fruit = grapefruit

Match a word from column A with a word from column B to make a compound word. Write each compound word on the lines below.

Column A

1. high — *Example*
2. rail
3. home
4. pea
5. sun
6. base
7. toe
8. sail
9. side
10. play
11. her
12. tooth

Column B

1. shine
2. work
3. boat
4. way
5. nail
6. nut
7. road
8. walk
9. brush
10. self
11. ball
12. ground

1. highway *Example*
2. _____
3. _____
4. _____
5. _____
6. _____

7. _____
8. _____
9. _____
10. _____
11. _____
12. _____

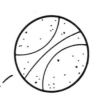

Compound Words

Add one word to each group of words below to form a compound word with each of the words in the group.

her		base		ear	
him	self *Example*	basket	_____	back	_____
your		snow		head	
fire		every		hand	
mail	_____	any	_____	lithe	_____
milk		no		win	
sail		to		half	
speed	_____	Sun	_____	running	_____
motor		birth		quarter	
in		pocket		rose	
be	_____	note	_____	balsa	_____
out		cook		fruit	
drive		flash		card	
high	_____	day	_____	black	_____
free		stop		back	
school		some		some	
class	_____	noon	_____	any	_____
bed		day		every	

Synonyms

Synonyms are words that have the same or nearly the same meaning.

last and final   mistake and error

Which word in the parentheses (   ) means the same as the word on the left? Write the word on the line in the mailbox.

Example →

Synonyms

1.	small and	1. little	1. (large, little, round)
2.	close and	2. _____	2. (easy, far, near)
3.	sad and	3. _____	3. (unhappy, glad, nice)
4.	bright and	4. _____	4. (dull, brilliant, clean)
5.	false and	5. _____	5. (clear, true, wrong)
6.	large and	6. _____	6. (little, lamp, huge)
7.	gift and	7. _____	7. (give, present, store)
8.	fast and	8. _____	8. (fresh, tame, quick)
9.	tidy and	9. _____	9. (neat, seed, near)
10.	stone and	10. _____	10. (store, rock, circle)
11.	fat and	11. _____	11. (tall, square, plump)
12.	raise and	12. _____	12. (lower, lift, carry)

cap / hat

Name _____

Synonyms

Synonyms are words that have the same or nearly the same meaning.

Select a synonym for the underlined word in the sentences below from the words in the Word Bank. Write the synonym on the line following the sentence.

Word Bank			
small	price	put	large
under	error	arrive	over
talk	sick	scared	robber
	reduce	mix	

Example > Susie <u>dashed</u> across the street. _____ran_____

1. The dog was <u>below</u> the chair. _____
2. Tom <u>placed</u> his book on the table. _____
3. The <u>huge</u> animal was in a cage. _____
4. The <u>burglar</u> stole a lot of money. _____
5. The clock was <u>above</u> the desk. _____
6. The loud noise <u>frightened</u> the baby. _____
7. I made a <u>mistake</u> on my test. _____
8. The <u>cost</u> was $1.00 for the notebook. _____
9. The child became <u>ill</u> at school. _____
10. I ordered a <u>little</u> pizza. _____
11. Please <u>come</u> to my party at 7:00 P.M. _____
12. Will you <u>speak</u> to the class? _____
13. Dad needs to <u>lessen</u> his work load. _____
14. You need to <u>blend</u> the eggs and sugar. _____

Grammar IF8730   4   © 1990 Instructional Fair, Inc.

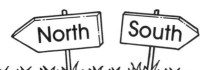

Antonyms

Antonyms are words that have opposite meanings.

Select an antonym for the underlined words in the sentences below from the words in the Word Bank. Write the antonym on the line following each sentence.

Word Bank

unbolt	strong	purchase	cooked
sharp	evil	ancient	assemble
minor	present	praised	learned
disarray	increase	day	

Example > The salesperson was courteous. ___rude___

1. The old man was feeble. _____
2. The castle was modern inside. _____
3. Caroline likes raw carrots. _____
4. The character in the book was good. _____
5. She taught Spanish every day. _____
6. Doug was absent yesterday. _____
7. The knife was dull and rusty. _____
8. The teacher criticized the student. _____
9. Lock the door, please. _____
10. The meeting will adjourn soon. _____
11. It was a major decision. _____
12. I am going to sell shoes. _____
13. You should decrease your sugar intake. _____
14. We went fishing in the middle of the night. _____
15. The room was in great order. _____

Synonyms-Antonyms Review

in | inside | out

Write a synonym and an antonym for each key word.

Answers will vary.

Synonym	Key Word	Antonym
Example > _entire_____	whole	_part_____
_____	quick	_____
_____	stay	_____
_____	small	_____
_____	near	_____
_____	loud	_____
_____	glad	_____
_____	dirty	_____
_____	difficult	_____
_____	wet	_____
_____	same	_____
_____	ill	_____
_____	repair	_____
_____	finish	_____
_____	depart	_____
_____	begin	_____
_____	high	_____
_____	large	_____
_____	shut	_____
_____	kind	_____
_____	smart	_____

Homonyms

Words that are pronounced the same, but their meanings and their spellings are not the same, are called homonyms.

Read the homonyms in the parentheses (   ). Write one of the homonyms in a blank in each sentence.

 **Example**

(two-to)

We have ___two___ apples.

We went ___to___ the store.

 **(pear-pair-) pare**

I ate the delicious _____ .

I have a _____ of gloves.

Will you _____ the peaches?

 **(sun-son)**

They have a _____ and a daughter.

The _____ is shining today.

 (ate-eight)

I _____ a pizza for lunch.

I bought _____ pencils.

(red-read)

I _____ the book.

My book is _____ .

 (one-won)

I _____ the race.

I have _____ brother.

Name _____

Homonyms

The sail is blue.
~~sale~~ ~~blew~~

Homonyms are words that sound the same, but have different spellings and meanings.

In the sentences below, circle the correct word.

Example ▷ We used (flower, (flour)) in our cake.

1. We went (to, too, two) the store.
2. The pig's (tale, tail) was short.
3. The (knight, night) rode a beautiful horse.
4. I have a (soar, sore) on my knee.
5. Mother said, "Please do not (waste, waist) time."
6. We had rare (steak, stake) for dinner.
7. We can (beet, beat) your team playing baseball.
8. Did you (rap, wrap) the present?
9. Do not run down the (stairs, stares).
10. Let's (paws, pause) for a drink of water.
11. Are you going to (wait, weight) for me?
12. I'm taking a (course, coarse) in English.
13. Have you (scene, seen) my science book?
14. The (sum, some) of the problem is 10.
15. Which soda did you (chews, choose)?
16. May I have a (piece, peace) of cake?
17. I have sand in my (pale, pail).
18. Please come to (hour, our) house.
19. My (aunt, ant) and uncle took us to the zoo.
20. Did you tie a square (not, knot)?

Name _____

Homonyms

There are four homonyms in each of the silly sentences.
Rewrite each sentence using the correct words.

Example > The bare eight for pairs.
The bear ate four pears. _____

1. I wood like the hole piece of stake.

    _____

2. Isle where my blew genes tomorrow.

    _____

3. Hour male is knot do today.

    _____

4. Last knight we one for sense.

    _____

5. Inn to daze we go on our crews.

    _____

6. Next weak my ant mite come hear.

    _____

7. My sun will by knew close.

    _____

8. The plain witch flu bye was noisy.

    _____

9. Ewe weight write near the gait.

    _____

10. Eye sea my deer friend nose you.

Prefixes

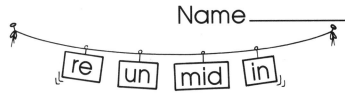

New words may be made from other words. One way to build a new word is to add a part to the beginning of a word.

Part	+	word	=	new word	
re	+	place	=	replace	(do again)
un	+	even	=	uneven	(not)
mid	+	air	=	midair	(middle)
in	+	different	=	indifferent	(not)

Use one of the above prefixes to write a new word that means the same as the description below.

Example > in the middle of <u>summer</u>   midsummer _____

1. <u>paint</u> again   _____

2. not <u>fair</u>   _____

3. not <u>complete</u>   _____

4. <u>mount</u> again   _____

5. not <u>touched</u>   _____

6. <u>wind</u> again   _____

7. not <u>clear</u>   _____

8. <u>do</u> again   _____

9. not <u>direct</u>   _____

10. not <u>fit</u>   _____

11. in the middle of the <u>day</u>   _____

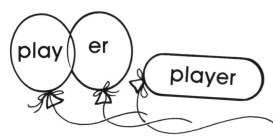

Suffixes

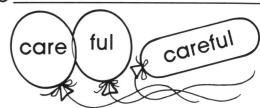

Another way to build a new word is to add a part at the end of the word.

word	+	**part**	=	**new word**	
sing	+	er	=	singer	(a person or thing who does something)
care	+	less	=	careless	(without)
skill	+	ful	=	skillful	(full of)

Use one of the above suffixes to write a new word for the underlined word that means the same as the description.

Example> one who can <u>jump</u>   <u>jumper</u>

1. full of <u>wonder</u>   _____

2. without <u>hope</u>   _____

3. full of <u>grace</u>   _____

4. without <u>worth</u>   _____

5. one who can <u>clean</u>   _____

6. full of <u>success</u>   _____

7. without <u>use</u>   _____

8. one who can <u>read</u>   _____

9. without <u>help</u>   _____

10. one who can <u>teach</u>   _____

11. full of <u>cheer</u>   _____

Name _____

Prefixes
Suffixes   Review

In each sentence below, find a word with a prefix or a suffix.
Circle the root word. Draw a line under the prefix or the suffix.

Example > The dentist said it would be (pain)less.

Example > My washing machine has a pre(soak) cycle.

1. Every sentence should be meaningful.
2. Do not be careless about your clothes.
3. I need to redo my report.
4. The grizzly bear gave a frightful roar.
5. My misfortune was breaking my arm.
6. The gardener began planting seeds in May.
7. The recipe said to precook the meat.
8. Did you unlock your suitcase?
9. In our city, the weather is changeable.
10. Wendy started preschool last September.
11. Andrew has a collection of wooden soldiers.
12. We live midway between New York and Boston.
13. My grandparents are inactive.
14. The painter needed a ladder for the ceiling.
15. Make the check payable to Dr. Weaver.
16. My new kitchen chairs are uncomfortable
17. The table had a washable surface.
18. I think I'm predestined to be a teacher.
19. That newspaper reporter seems hotheaded!
20. The trapeze artist appeared to be fearless.

Capital Letters

The first word of every sentence must begin with a capital letter.

Use the words in the **Word Bank** to complete each sentence.

Word Bank				
seven	trains	do	snow	presents
apples	blue	dogs	airplanes	clowns
	pair		coats	

Example 〉 <u>Twelve</u> __ inches make a foot.

1. _____ are my favorite animals.

2. _____ days are in a week.

3. _____ are round and red.

4. _____ run on tracks.

5. _____ fly in the sky.

6. _____ is the color of the sky.

7. _____ means to have two.

8. _____ you have any brothers?

9. _____ make me laugh.

10. _____ falls in the winter.

11. _____ keep us warm.

12. _____ are fun to open.

Name_____

Capital Letters

Use capital letters for names of people and pets. Use a capital letter to begin each word in a name.

Steven Alan Jones   **Donald Duck**
Lisa Marie Hayes   **Minnie Mouse**

Copy these names. Use capital letters where needed.

1. jane ellen smith <u>Jane Ellen Smith</u> *Example*

2. mickey mouse _____

3. paul mark cooper _____

4. mary sue ford _____

5. snoopy _____

6. david joseph moore _____

7. nancy lynn parker _____

8. charlie brown _____

9. kenny david gibson _____

10. tom edward turner _____

11. lassie _____

12. sara jane post _____

13. louisa mae williams _____

14. tabby _____

Capital Letters

Use a capital letter for a title in a name. Use a period after the abbreviation.

Mr. Sam Tucker   **Dr. Helen Jean Bayer**

Use a capital letter for an initial in a name. Use a period after the initial.

Tony L. Carter   **Jill C. Dolan**

Copy these sentences. Use capital letters and periods where needed.

1. mr jack m kent is my friend.

   _____

2. dr robert e lewis is my doctor.

   _____

3. mrs ann s sharp is my mother.

   _____

4. mindy gave me a minnie mouse coloring book.

   _____

5. george washington was our first president.

   _____

6. karen's dad is mr mark p simon.

   _____

7. my teacher is mr vincent r williams.

Name _____

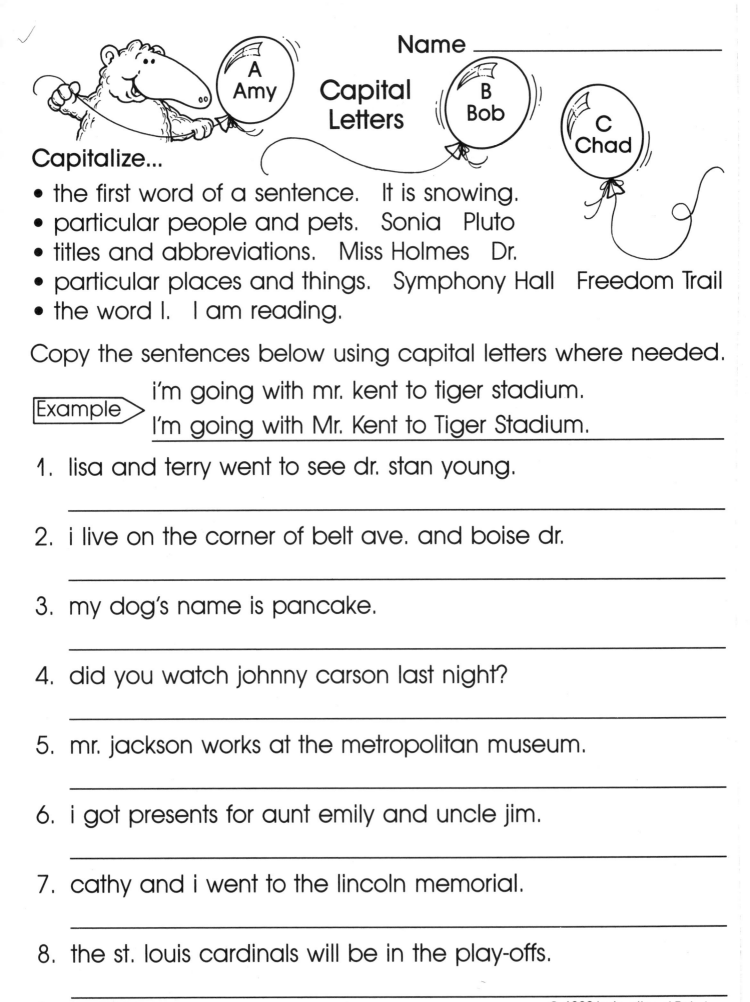

Capital Letters

Capitalize...
- the first word of a sentence.   It is snowing.
- particular people and pets.   Sonia   Pluto
- titles and abbreviations.   Miss Holmes   Dr.
- particular places and things.   Symphony Hall   Freedom Trail
- the word I.   I am reading.

Copy the sentences below using capital letters where needed.

Example ▷   i'm going with mr. kent to tiger stadium.
             I'm going with Mr. Kent to Tiger Stadium.
             _____

1. lisa and terry went to see dr. stan young.

   _____

2. i live on the corner of belt ave. and boise dr.

   _____

3. my dog's name is pancake.

   _____

4. did you watch johnny carson last night?

   _____

5. mr. jackson works at the metropolitan museum.

   _____

6. i got presents for aunt emily and uncle jim.

   _____

7. cathy and i went to the lincoln memorial.

   _____

8. the st. louis cardinals will be in the play-offs.

   _____

Capital Letters

Names of months, special days and holidays begin with capital letters.

January New Year's Day /Example/			
1.	2.	3.	4.
5.	6.	7.	8.
9.	10.	11.	12.

Rewrite these months, special days and holidays. Put them on the calendar in order. Use capital letters where needed.

1. january—new year's day
   martin luther king day

2. february—valentine's day

3. march—st. patrick's day

4. april—april fool's day
   easter

5. may—memorial day
   mother's day

6. june—flag day
   father's day

7. july—independence day

8. august—friendship day

9. september—labor day

10. october—columbus day
    halloween
    united nations day

11. november—thanksgiving
    veteran's day

12. december—christmas
    hanukkah

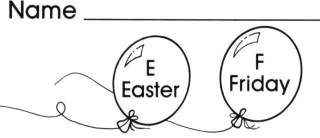

Capital Letters

Capitalize...

- cities, states, countries.   Tulsa, Oklahoma, United States
- lakes, rivers, oceans.   Blue River   Indian Ocean
- holidays.   Thanksgiving
- days of the week and months.   Monday   June
- names for people of particular countries.   French

Copy the sentences below using capital letters where needed.

Example > The third sunday in june is father's day.
The third Sunday in June is Father's Day.

1. The mississippi river is east of st. louis, missouri.

   _____

2. Many spanish people live in houston, texas.

   _____

3. Valentine's day is celebrated february 14th.

   _____

4. School starts the first tuesday after labor day.

   _____

5. I swam in lake michigan when I was in chicago, illinois.

   _____

6. I visited london, england last july.

   _____

7. hoover dam and lake mead are near las vegas.

   _____

8. Last monday, august 17, was my birthday.

   _____

Capital Letters

Capitalize most words in a book title. Always capitalize the first word and the last word. Do not capitalize little words, such as: the, in, to, at.

The Fox and the Hound

Write one of the following book titles on each book.

the egg and i
railroads of the world
cinderella
cat in the hat
jack and the beanstalk

goldilocks and the three bears
the story of george washington
alice in wonderland
how to write reports
jokes and riddles

Example

The Egg and I

Capital Letters

Capitalize...

- titles of T.V. programs, movies, books and poems except for small words like: and, of, in, the. Always capitalize the first and last words.   Dungeons and Dragons

- Copy the title below the book, T.V. screen or movie screen using capital letters where needed.

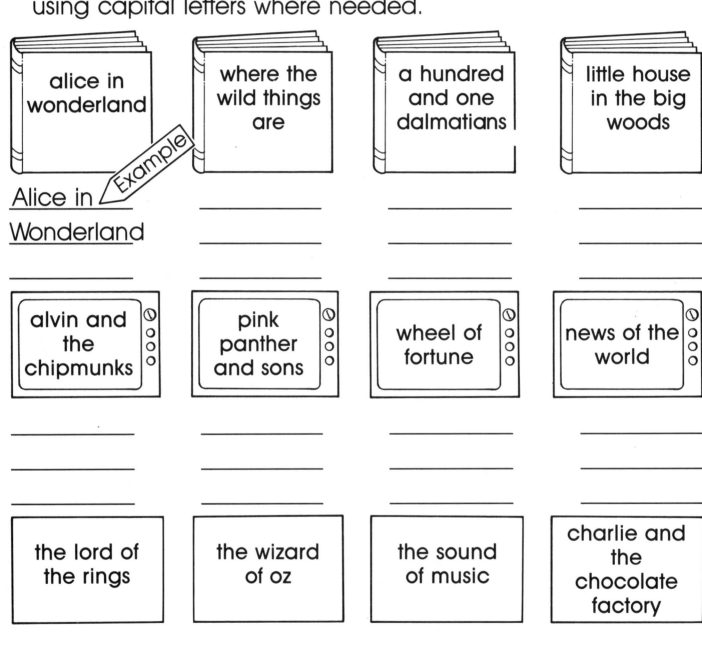

Books:
- alice in wonderland — *Example* — Alice in Wonderland
- where the wild things are
- a hundred and one dalmatians
- little house in the big woods

T.V. screens:
- alvin and the chipmunks
- pink panther and sons
- wheel of fortune
- news of the world

Movie screens:
- the lord of the rings
- the wizard of oz
- the sound of music
- charlie and the chocolate factory

Name _____

Capital Letters

Review

All About Me

Complete each sentence using capital letters where needed. Don't forget the periods.

1. My name is _____

2. The date I was born is _____

3. I live in the city of _____ in the state

   of _____ in the country of_____

4. My favorite book is _____

5. My favorite holiday is _____

6. My favorite pet's name is _____

7. My favorite movie is _____

8. My best friend is _____

9. My favorite teacher is _____

10. My favorite day of the week is _____ because

    _____

11. My favorite song is _____

12. The names of my family members are:

    _____   _____   _____

    _____   _____   _____

Capital Letters

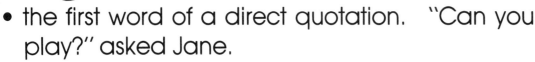

Capitalize...

- the first word of a direct quotation. "Can you play?" asked Jane.
- the first word in a greeting of a letter. Dear Ned,
- The first word in the closing of a letter. Your friend, Tracy

Copy the sentences below using capital letters where needed.

Example > My letter began, "dear aunt carol."
          My letter began, "Dear Aunt Carol."

1. Dad said, "barry, let's play ball."

_____

2. The teacher asked, "have you finished your homework?"

_____

3. My note ended, "your friend, nina."

_____

4. "that's it," said Sean. "that's the right answer."

_____

5. Mother's note to my teacher began, "dear miss black."

_____

6. "i got a new bike!" yelled Erik.

_____

7. The thank you note ended, "gratefully, mrs. shea."

_____

8. I whispered, "be quiet, the baby is sleeping."

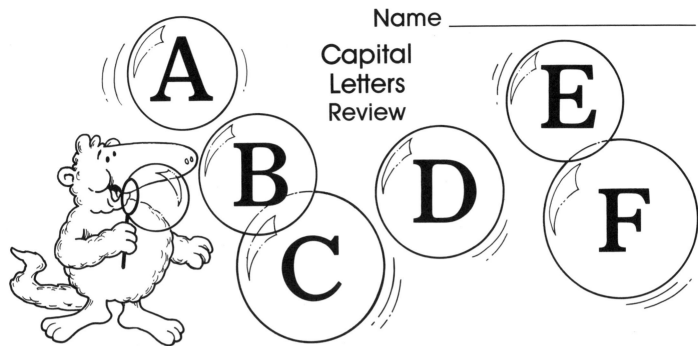

Capital
Letters
Review

In the sentences below, circle the words that should begin with a capital letter.

Example ➤ is "i love lucy" still on television?

1. "after lunch," said sue, "let's go shopping."

2. i learned a lot from the book, *inside the personal computer*.

3. my class from hudson school went to forest park.

4. carlos speaks spanish, french and english.

5. the carter family lives on terrace drive.

6. "the new kid on the block" is a great story.

7. we saw the movie "ghostbusters" last saturday.

8. christopher columbus discovered america in 1492.

9. i was born june 12, 1965, in denver, colorado.

10. next thursday, mr. and mrs. evans have an anniversary.

11. my brother will attend harvard college in boston.

12. the letter to montie ended, "love from, aunt rose."

13. in hawaii, kamehameka day is celebrated each june.

14. mrs. hardy said, "don't be late for the party."

15. stone brothers hardware is on elm street.

Sentences

This is my bone.

A sentence is a group of words that tells a complete idea.

The dictionaries are on the bottom shelf.

Not all groups of words are sentences. This group of words does not tell a complete idea.

The dictionaries on the bottom shelf

If the group of words below tells a complete idea, write **S** for sentence on the line. If it does not tell a complete idea, write **NS** for not a sentence. Add periods if the group of words is a sentence.

Example> ____S____ Carla ate her dinner.

Example> ____NS____ After the ballgame

1. _____ The grass is green

2. _____ The English test tomorrow

3. _____ After the ballgame

4. _____ The blue sweater in my drawer

5. _____ It is snowing

6. _____ Matt and Jimmy are twins

7. _____ Under the desk my cat

8. _____ Derek visited Mexico

9. _____ The puzzle on the table

10. _____ Julie dressed her doll

24

Sentences

Remember: A sentence contains a complete thought.

For each group of words below, write a complete sentence, putting the words in the correct order.

Answers will vary.

Example > squirrel tree the gray our in little lives
The little gray squirrel lives in our tree.

1. a in tied Billy knot string the

_____

2. brought party each something the child for

_____

3. children street on the play kickball my

_____

4. student new this is year Joanie a

_____

5. favorite red my roses are flowers bright

_____

6. new dentist gave toothbrush the me a

_____

7. was with steak mushrooms our served brown

_____

8. my took cleaners the I coat to

_____

9. ticket name the it had lucky Susie's on

_____

25

Sentences

A sentence is a group of words that contains a complete thought.

Every sentence has two parts. The **subject** tells who or what did something. The **predicate** tells what the subject does or did, or what the subject is or has.

Rachel	has a new bike.
who	**has**
The Drama Club	meets every Wednesday.
what	**does**

In the sentences below, draw one line under the subject and two lines under the predicate.

The snowman is melting.

Example > Cats are furry and soft.

1. The horses are racing to the finish line.
2. Mrs. Porter went to see Jack's teacher.
3. Josh moved to Atlanta, Georgia.
4. Monica's birthday is July 15th.
5. The ball rolled into the street.
6. The policeman stopped the traffic.
7. Tammy planned a surprise party.
8. The winning team received a trophy.
9. The fireworks displays were fantastic.
10. The heavy rain drove everyone inside.
11. Adam looked everywhere for his book.
12. Can you hear the band outside?
13. Bob and Andy have just moved here.
14. All of the team is going to the soccer tournament.
15. My family has tickets for the football game.

Sentences
Subjects Predicates

Every sentence has two parts which are called **subject** and **predicate**. The **subject** tells who or what does something. The **predicate** tells what the subject does, what the subject is or what the subject has.

The train	goes on tracks.
what	does

That song	is my favorite.
what	is

My friend	has new ice skates.
who	has

In the sentences below, draw one line under the subject and two lines under the predicate.

Example > The cows are in the pasture.

1. The telephone was for me.

2. Mother baked a pumpkin pie.

3. Alison fed the baby animals.

4. The Indians passed the peace pipe.

5. The garden needs water to grow.

6. Lisa has beautiful long hair.

7. Doug and Ben played tennis.

8. Our family went apple picking.

9. The washing machine was broken.

10. My grandparents called me on my birthday.

11. Alex bought a new computer game.

12. We went on a float trip last summer.

27

Sentences
Subjects   Predicates

Review

Write a complete sentence using each of the following subjects.

Example> Miss Piggy likes purple gloves _____ .

1. The bears _____ .

2. The tunnel _____ .

3. Stan _____ .

4. My camera _____ .

5. Snoopy _____ .

6. Dana and Andrea _____ .

7. Thanksgiving _____ .

Write a complete sentence using each of the following predicates.

Example> The banana split _____ was wonderful.

1. _____ made me laugh.

2. _____ is ten miles away.

3. _____ plays the piano.

4. _____ grows very well.

5. _____ woke up the campers.

6. _____ was brand new.

7. _____ are bright red.

28

Sentences
Subject/Predicate   Review

Write a complete sentence using each of the following subjects.

Example > The magician <u>performs difficult tricks</u> _____ .

1. The truck _____ .

2. Mr. and Mrs. Turner _____ .

3. The clowns _____ .

4. Fresh strawberries _____ .

5. Our team _____ .

6. A large crowd _____ .

7. Pancakes _____ .

8. All of the joggers _____ .

9. The skeleton _____ .

Write a complete sentence using each of the following predicates.

Example > _____ The busy street _____ was noisy.

1. _____ was funny.

2. _____ will be ready.

3. _____ went too quickly.

4. _____ is on the corner.

5. _____ were ruined.

6. _____ still exists.

7. _____ was fun.

8. _____ were on my desk.

9. _____ turned to gold.

29

Sentences

A sentence must answer these two questions.

Who or what did something? What happened?

> Robert forgot his lunch.

Not all groups of words are sentences.
> Forgot his lunch

Decide if each of the following groups of words answers both questions; who or what did something and what happened. After each group of words write **S** for sentence or **NS** for not a sentence. Add a period if it is a sentence.

Example > The largest tigers in the world   <u>NS</u>

Example > We will visit Mexico.   <u>S</u>

1. The present was wrapped   _____

2. Andrea swam very fast   _____

3. A very funny comic book   _____

4. Found and buried the nut   _____

5. They ride horses   _____

6. A speedboat on the lake   _____

7. On Saturday, around the house   _____

8. That joke was not funny   _____

9. Lost her favorite ring at the store   _____

10. During the Middle Ages, Robin Hood   _____

11. Finally finished the job   _____

12. The rocket landed yesterday   _____

13. The tiny baby lying quietly in the cradle   _____

*On the back of your paper, rewrite the groups of words that were not sentences so they contain a complete thought.

Sentences
Statement or Question?

Each kind of sentence does a different job. A statement is a sentence that tells something. It ends with a period.

I study French.

A question is a sentence that asks something. It ends with a question mark.

Do you study French?

Decide if each sentence below is a statement or a question. Write the answer on the line. Put the correct ending mark at the end of each sentence.

| Example> | Did you finish your homework? | question |
| Example> | Our grass needs cutting. | statement |

1. Our company is coming soon   1. _____

2. Sarah wore a heavy sweater   2. _____

3. Is that your lunchbox   3. _____

4. May I have some popcorn   4. _____

5. The music was too loud   5. _____

6. When is your birthday   6. _____

7. Have you seen Erik   7. _____

8. I need a map to get home   8. _____

9. Where is your notebook   9. _____

10. I need $1.00 for lunch   10. _____

31

Jan, what are you eating?

I'm eating a cookie.

Questions
Statements

In each picture are two children. Give them each a name. Write a question one child might be asking the other. Place a question mark after each question.

Write the answer of the second child. Place a period after your answer.

Names: _____ and _____

Question: _____

Answer: _____

U.S. MAIL

Names: _____ and _____

Question: _____

Answer: _____

Names: _____ and _____

Question: _____

Answer: _____

TRICK

Names: _____ and _____

Question: _____

Answer: _____

On another sheet of paper, write 5 questions for a friend to answer.

Sentences
Exclamation or Command?

A command is a sentence that tells someone to do something. A command ends with a period.

Stop talking. | • |

An exclamation is a sentence that shows strong feelings, such as anger or excitement. It ends with an exclamation point.

This is so wonderful! | ! |

Decide if each sentence below is a command or an exclamation. Write your answer on the line. Put the correct ending mark at the end of each sentence.

Example> Jill, feed the dog.   command _____

Example> I hate peas!   exclamation _____

1. Don't be late for your lesson   1. _____

2. Answer the door   2. _____

3. This water is too hot   3. _____

4. Tony, make your bed   4. _____

5. It's freezing in here   5. _____

6. Get up at 7:00 a.m. tomorrow   6. _____

7. Your grades are marvelous   7. _____

8. Hang up your clothes   8. _____

9. This surprise party is great   9. _____

10. Those elephants are enormous   10. _____

Can you play?

Hurry up!

I ate an apple.

Question Marks
Periods
Exclamation Points

A period is used...

- at the end of statements and commands.
- after an initial in a name.
- after many abbreviations.

We went home.
F.D. Roosevelt
Dr. Ave. in. Co.

A question mark is used...

- at the end of a question.   Did you mail my letter?

An exclamation point is used...

- after an exclamation or command that shows

  strong feelings.   Come quickly!

In the following sentences, use periods, question marks and exclamation points where they are needed.

| Example | Lt. Stanley R. Mayberry is my uncle.

1. Thurs , Sept 7, is my birthday
2. My neighbor works at J C Penney Co
3. Can you run a mi in 15 minutes
4. Will you take a train to St Louis
5. Eat your dinner
6. The room measured 25 ft 4 in in length
7. Did Carla move to Price Dr last July
8. Main St and 5th Ave is where Sara lives
9. Hurry up and finish that right now
10. Rev and Mrs R W Gordon live next door
11. I bought a doz apples for Ms Haley
12. My appointment with Dr Rosen is at 2:30 P M
13. The baby was born at 6 A M and weighed 9 lbs 13 oz

Name_____

Common Nouns

A noun is a word that names a:

person  or place  or thing

Fill in each blank with a noun.

1. My _____ was barking.

2. I like _____ to eat.

3. _____ is extremely cold.

4. A _____ has many colors.

5. The red _____ is pretty.

6. The living room _____ is on.

7. John rode the _____ to school.

8. Sally read her favorite _____.

9. She had a _____ on her face.

10. I sat in a comfortable _____.

11. I play the _____ well.

12. The _____ captured the robber.

13. Bob played outside in the _____.

Name_____

Proper Nouns

A noun that names a particular person, place or thing is a proper noun. Proper nouns begin with capital letters.

Dr. John Smith   **Mulberry Street**   **Mount Everest**

Read the following sentences. Write the proper nouns from each sentence on the scoreboard below. Be sure to begin each proper noun with a capital letter.

1. My friend, carol, is from houston, texas.

2. I sent a letter to uncle charlie.

3. I watched mister ed on television.

4. The lincoln memorial is in washington d c.

5. My aunt mary took me to see "star wars".

6. In 1492, columbus discovered america.

7. Our first president was george washington.

8. I live on fifth street in new york.

9. I saw dr. tom holmes when I was sick.

10. We camped in yellowstone national park.

SCOREBOARD				
1. *Example* Carol Houston Texas	2.	3.	4.	5.
6.	7.	8.	9.	10.

Common Nouns
Proper Nouns

A common noun names a person, place or thing.
A common noun begins with a small letter.

dog   **book**

A proper noun names a particular person, place or thing.
A proper noun begins with a capital letter.

Lassie   **Sleeping Beauty**

Copy each of the following nouns into a bubble from the common noun pipe or proper noun pipe.

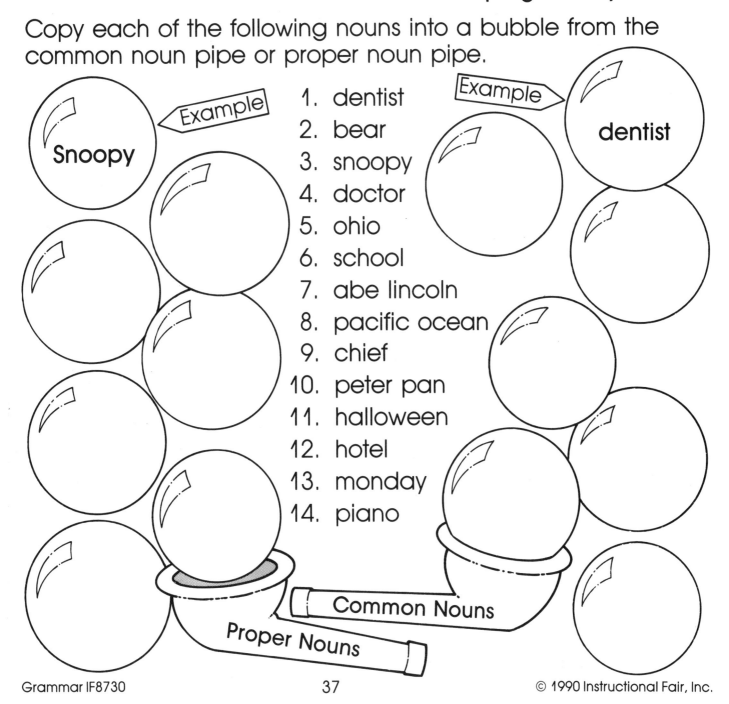

1. dentist
2. bear
3. snoopy
4. doctor
5. ohio
6. school
7. abe lincoln
8. pacific ocean
9. chief
10. peter pan
11. halloween
12. hotel
13. monday
14. piano

Snoopy

Example

Example

dentist

Common Nouns

Proper Nouns

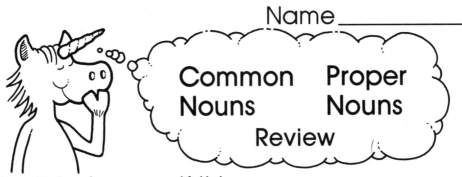

Name_____

Common Nouns   Proper Nouns
Review

Look at the list of nouns. If it is a **common noun**, copy it in the cloud titled common nouns. If it is a **proper noun**, change its first letters to capital letters and copy it in the cloud titled proper nouns.

1. ohio
2. dr simon
3. ocean
4. president lincoln
5. dog
6. jane
7. new york
8. ice cream
9. mount everest
10. columbus

11. teacher
12. second avenue
13. circus
14. sheriff

common nouns

proper nouns

Plural Nouns

A singular noun names one person, place or thing.

APPLE

A plural noun names more than one person, place or thing. Usually, plural nouns have an **S** ending.

APPLES

When a singular noun ends in **S-SH-CH- or X**, add **es** to make the plural form.

S—	losses	buses
SH—	brushes	bushes
CH—	peaches	bunches
X—	boxes	foxes

Write the plural of each of the following.

car	pencil	dress	dish	bird
_____	_____	_____	_____	_____

sandwich	six	balloon	ax	ball
_____	_____	_____	_____	_____

Name _____

Plural Nouns

To form the plural of most nouns, add **s**.

bananas    **chairs**

When the singular form ends with **s-sh-ch-x**, add **es**.

boxes 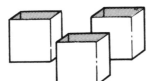   **peaches**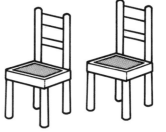

Write the plural for each of the nouns on the chalkboard.

bunch	class	wax	fox
chair	brush	watch	pronoun
bus	fix	light	bus
plant	radio	push	wish
clock	pass	tax	switch
dish	church	report	press
witch	trick	patch	ticket

__bunches__ **Example** _____ _____ _____

_____ _____ _____ _____

_____ _____ _____ _____

_____ _____ _____ _____

_____ _____ _____ _____

_____ _____ _____ _____

Plural Nouns

When a singular noun ends in a **consonant** and **y**, change the **y** to **i** and add **es**.

penny-pennies  fly-flies

Some singular nouns form their plural in special ways. There is no rule for these, so you have to memorize them.

man-men   **woman-women**   **child-children**
foot-feet   **tooth-teeth**   **mouse-mice**

Below is a chalkboard. Write the plural of each of the following words on the chalkboard.

1. bunny   5. mouse   9. man
2. pony   6. tooth   10. boy
3. foot   7. child   11. cherry
4. party   8. candy   12. woman

---

1. bunnies ◁ Example _____   7. _____

2. _____   8. _____

3. _____   9. _____

4. _____   10. _____

5. _____   11. _____

6. _____   12. _____

Plural Nouns

When a singular noun ends in a consonant and **y**, change the **y** to **i** and add **es**.

daisy
dais**ies**

butterfly
butterfl**ies**

To some nouns ending in **f**, simply add **s**.

chief-chie**fs**   bluff-bluf**fs**

To other nouns ending in **f** or **fe**, change the **f** or **fe** to **v** and add **es**. You must memorize these as there is no rule.

calf-cal**ves**   knife-kni**ves**   loaf-loa**ves**   life-li**ves**
wolf-wol**ves**   shelf-shel**ves**   half-hal**ves**   leaf-lea**ves**

Write the plural for each of the nouns below on the chalkboard.

1. dwarf
2. cherry
3. knife
4. roof
5. life
6. baby

7. calf
8. cuff
9. lady
10. wolf
11. half
12. belief

13. sky
14. leaf
15. army
16. fairy
17. shelf
18. loaf

1. dwarfs ◁ Example
2. _____
3. _____
4. _____
5. _____
6. _____

7. _____
8. _____
9. _____
10. _____
11. _____
12. _____

13. _____
14. _____
15. _____
16. _____
17. _____
18. _____

Plural
Nouns

These nouns are the same for both singular and plural. You will have to memorize them.

deer	salmon	trout	sheep	moose
tuna	cod	pike	bass	elk

These nouns form their plurals in special ways. You will have to memorize them.

goose-geese	man-men	woman-women	tooth-teeth
ox-oxen	foot-feet	child-children	mouse-mice

Write the plural for each of the nouns below on the blanks.

1. cod
2. goose
3. salmon
4. woman
5. moose
6. tooth

7. trout
8. elk
9. ox
10. deer
11. foot
12. pike

13. tuna
14. man
15. child
16. bass
17. mouse
18. sheep

1. cod _Example_ _____
2. _____
3. _____
4. _____
5. _____
6. _____

7. _____
8. _____
9. _____
10. _____
11. _____
12. _____

13. _____
14. _____
15. _____
16. _____
17. _____
18. _____

Name_____

Plural Nouns
Review

Follow the path around. Write the plural for each noun.

Start →

fish
_____

box
_____

party
_____

house
_____

clock
_____

baby
_____

lunch
_____

class
_____

pass
_____

mouse
_____

foot
_____

man
_____

broom
_____

pony
_____

wish
_____

board
_____

End

Name _____

Plural
Nouns

Review

Write the plural for each of the nouns below.

wish Example	hobby	sheep	day
wishes	_____	_____	_____
deer	bluff	child	boss
_____	_____	_____	_____
rash	cookie	match	knife
_____	_____	_____	_____
car	success	pony	foot
_____	_____	_____	_____
kiss	city	couch	mouse
_____	_____	_____	_____
woman	half	mirror	trout
_____	_____	_____	_____
person	tooth	dress	girl
_____	_____	_____	_____

Possessive Nouns

A possessive noun shows ownership or possession. To make a singular noun show possession, add an **apostrophe** and s.

child's toy   teacher's book

Fill in the blank with a possessive noun.

Example> the _dog's_____ bone

1. the _____ nest

2. the _____ cage

3. the _____ petal

4. the _____ nose

To make a plural noun that ends in **s** show possession, add an apostrophe after the s.

dogs' bones

To make a plural noun that does not end in **s** show possession, add an apostrophe and s.

children's games

Fill in each blank with a possessive noun.

Example> the _dogs'_____ tails

1. the _____ legs

2. the _____ hoses

3. the _____ tails

4. the _____ pages

Possessive Nouns

A possessive noun is a noun that shows ownership.

To make a singular noun show possession, add an apostrophe and **s**.

farmer's rake    garden's flower

If a plural noun ends in **s**, simply add an apostrophe.

farmers' rakes   gardens' flowers

If a plural noun does not end in **s**, add an apostrophe and **s**.

men's shoes   women's shoes

Write each group of words to make them show ownership.

Example > the report card of Paul   Paul's report card _____

1. the toys of the children   _____
2. the tail of the monkey   _____
3. the cages of the animals   _____
4. the balls of the bowlers   _____
5. the house of my friend   _____
6. the uniforms of the players   _____
7. the backpack of Joan   _____
8. the shoes of the runners   _____
9. the paintings of the artist   _____
10. the monitor of the computer   _____
11. the hats of the men   _____
12. the wife of my boss   _____

Possessive Nouns

dog's bones

dogs' bones

Change the underlined word to show possession by adding an apostrophe or apostrophe and s. Write the possessive form on the line.

	Possessive
Example> Sally dress is blue	Sally's
1. Mother took me to Tony house.	_____
2. The chickens eggs were large.	_____
3. Jonathan bicycle needs new brakes.	_____
4. Follow the team rules.	_____
5. The shoes soles need repair.	_____
6. Mrs. Thomas car was in the driveway.	_____
7. My brother story won first prize.	_____
8. Our neighbors lawns need cutting.	_____
9. Ellen paintings were on display.	_____
10. The truck drivers routes were long.	_____
11. The babies toys are put away.	_____
12. The principal office is small.	_____
13. The bird nest is completed.	_____
14. The doctors hours were long.	_____
15. The painter brushes were clean.	_____

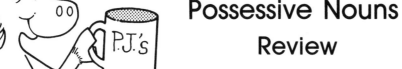

Possessive Nouns
Review

Change the underlined word to show possession by adding an apostrophe or apostrophe and s. Write the possessive form on the line.

| **possessive** |

Example⟩ The <u>balloon</u> string is long.   balloon's

1. The three <u>cats</u> paws were wet.   1. _____

2. <u>Mary</u> pencil was broken.   2. _____

3. Both <u>boys</u> grades were good.   3. _____

4. This house is <u>Cliff</u> house.   4. _____

5. <u>Tony</u> aunt came to visit.   5. _____

6. Some <u>flowers</u> leaves were large.   6. _____

7. We saw two <u>bears</u> tracks.   7. _____

8. The <u>children</u> room was messy.   8. _____

9. My <u>sister</u> birthday is today.   9. _____

10. The <u>clowns</u> acts made us laugh.   10. _____

11. Charlie Brown filled <u>Snoopy</u> dish.   11. _____

12. Mark joined the game with the <u>boys.</u>   12. _____

13. The baseball <u>players</u> uniforms are clean.   13. _____

14. The <u>dog</u> dish was empty.   14. _____

Verbs

Verbs are words that show action or say that something is.

We **sailed** on Lake Michigan.
I **am** ten years old.

In the sentences below, circle the verbs.

Example > We (went) to a movie.

1. Dad washed his new car in the driveway.
2. Nancy took pictures with her new camera.
3. We numbered our paper from 1 to 10.
4. My friends need help with their homework.
5. Mother answered the doorbell in her apron.
6. I lost my new sweater at the game.
7. The students did their math on the board.
8. We painted our house white and green.
9. Steve ran the 100-yard dash in the race.
10. The whole class laughed at my jokes.
11. The chef baked delicious pies and cakes.
12. Judy slipped on the ice and broke her arm.
13. Keith thought about his upcoming vacation.
14. Read the second chapter by tomorrow.
15. We looked through the microscope.
16. The boys ran and jumped over the fence.
17. The squirrels looked at us and then ran away.
18. Math is the subject most difficult for me.
19. My twin sisters are in the seventh grade.
20. My family was in Colorado when our car quit!

$$\begin{array}{r} 4 \\ \times\,3 \\ \hline 12 \end{array} \qquad \begin{array}{l} 12-6=6 \\ \\ 172 \\ +\,18 \\ \hline 190 \end{array}$$

Action Verbs

Action verbs tell what a person or thing does.

Birds fly.   Dogs run.

Some action verbs tell about actions you can see. Others tell about actions you cannot see.

I enjoyed the game.   We liked the show.

Circle the action verbs. Write them on the lines below.

1. raced	8. threw	15. sped	22. roared
2. traveled	9. went	16. popcorn	23. tiny
3. moon	10. player	17. adored	24. swam
4. viewed	11. divided	18. door	25. way
5. car	12. sewed	19. ruler	26. cried
6. sang	13. tennis	20. driver	27. worked
7. go	14. people	21. paints	28. eraser

_____   _____   _____   _____

_____   _____   _____   _____

_____   _____   _____   _____

Helping Verbs

A helping verb is used with an action verb. The most important verb is called the main verb and usually comes last. All the other words in the verb are called helping verbs.

helping verbs	main verb
was	turning
should have	turned
must have been	turning

Study this wheel of helping verbs.

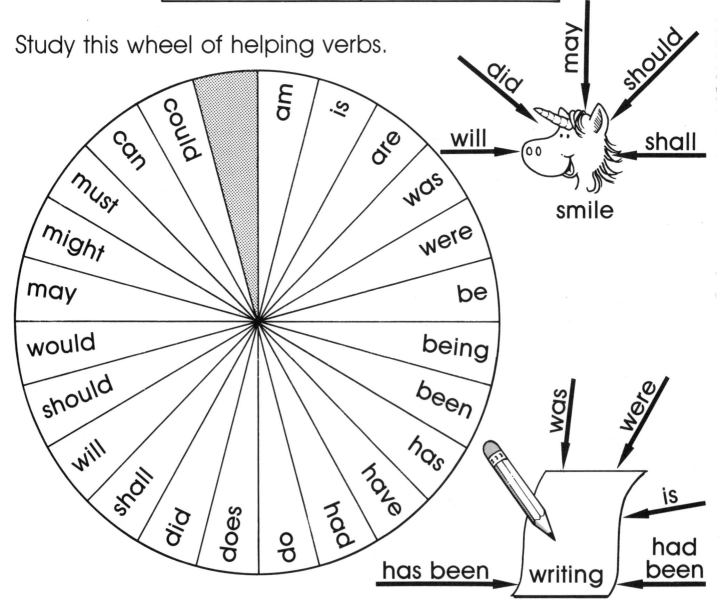

On the back of this paper, write ten sentences using helping verbs. Do not use a helping verb more than once.

Helping Verbs

A verb may be a single word or a group of words. A verb with more than one word is made of a **main verb** and one or more **helping verbs**.

These words are **often** used as **helping verbs**		These verbs are **always** used as **helping verbs**	
am	have	can	may
is	has	could	might
are	had		
was	do	will	shall
were	does	would	should
did			

In the following sentences, underline the main verb once and the helping verbs twice.

Today, I may read in class.

Example ▷ I <u>may</u> <u>have</u> <u>won</u> first prize.

1. Maria might spend the night.
2. The flowers are growing tall.
3. Matt is playing the piano for the play.
4. They were going to the movie.
5. Freddie should listen in class.
6. Lori should have eaten her vegetables.
7. I will be twelve on my next birthday.
8. I can do my homework later.
9. Vince has been working much too hard.
10. When are you going to finish the book?

53

Helping Verbs

Usually verbs that end in **en** or **ing** need helping verbs.

I **have** writt**en**.      I **am** writ**ing**.

In the following sentences, underline the main verb with one line. Underline the helping verbs with two lines.

Example > I have been swimming.

1. We were going to the tennis match.

2. The children have eaten lunch already.

3. They must have been sleeping soundly.

4. We could go to the circus on Saturday.

5. Uncle Harry has driven to Houston.

6. You are playing the piano very well.

7. Barry was studying for the test.

8. Chocolate sauce will be added to the dessert.

9. Jan has gone to the concert.

10. I am planning a party for my mother.

11. They have decided on a name for the baby.

12. Wendy may be riding her bike to school.

13. Carl and Gary should be coming soon.

14. I have been cutting the grass.

Helping Verbs

Always use helping verbs with **been, seen, done, gone**.

They **have been** ice skating.

Sometimes helping verbs and main verbs are separated by words that are not verbs.

Mike **can** usually **win** in Scrabble.

In the following sentences, underline the main verb once and the helping verbs twice.

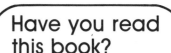

I have done well on my test.

Example > My brother <u>can</u>not <u>drive</u> yet.

1. Have you seen my new car?
2. Carlos did not tell anyone his secret.
3. I am usually working on Saturday.
4. Debbie has gone to the meeting at school.
5. She is not going swimming in the lake.
6. You should never chew gum in class.
7. Frank cannot get his locker open.
8. Did your older sister marry Tom?
9. I have been to my violin lesson.
10. I might not finish the large pizza.
11. Does the basketball game start at noon?
12. Tim can only play for one hour.
13. Was your mother angry about the window?
14. I am usually able to babysit on weekends.
15. I have never been to Hawaii, but I want to go!
16. Teaching school has always been my ambition.
17. Sara can often finish her homework before dinner.
18. Writing books is an enormous amount of work.

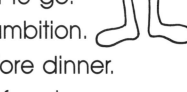

Have you read this book?

Verbs
Review

Underline the **whole verb** in each sentence below.

Example ▷ We <u>should be cooking</u> dinner now.

1. The music was loud in the room.

2. Leon has been watering the grass.

3. Pedro has gone to school for four years.

4. We stood for the National Anthem.

5. Jill has eaten all the popcorn.

6. Katie and Julie are twins.

7. They have collected money for needy children.

8. Mary Lou will keep her cat inside.

9. Read the directions on the cover.

Circle the correct verb in each sentence below.

Example ▷ Martin (am, (is)) my neighbor.

1. You (were, was) excellent in the talent show.

2. Maria and Joanie (are, was) going to the zoo.

3. The policeman (is, are) directing traffic.

4. I (was, is) eating pizza.

5. Craig (be, has been) packing for his trip.

6. I (is, am) doing a puzzle for my project.

7. The birds (was, were) singing outside my window.

8. The children (are, is) dressing up for Halloween.

56

Present Tense Verbs

Review

Write the correct spelling for each verb in the clouds so it will show present tense. Use the **s** form.

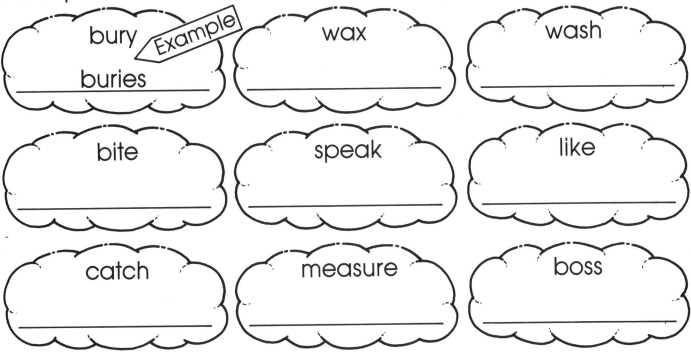

bury *Example* →

buries _____

wax

_____

wash

_____

bite

_____

speak

_____

like

_____

catch

_____

measure

_____

boss

_____

In the sentences below, circle the correct form of the verb.

Example → Jackie (carry, (carries)) her purse to school.

1. My father (shave, shaves) every day.

2. The chorus (sing, sings) beautifully.

3. The ice cream cones (taste, tastes) delicious.

4. My neighbor (teach, teaches) French.

5. Meg (dash, dashes) to school every day.

6. The birds (fly, flies) from tree to tree.

7. Elm Street (cross, crosses) Main Street.

8. Michael and Keith (play, plays) tennis.

9. They (wait, waits) for the bus at the corner.

10. The clowns (make, makes) us laugh.

Grammar IF8730   57

Past Tense Verbs

You can make most verbs tell about the past by adding **ed** to the basic form.

       walk-walked   talk-talked

Sometimes you must make spelling changes.

When the verb ends in a silent **e**, drop the **e**, add **ed**.

       rake-raked   hope-hoped

When the verb ends in **y** after a consonant, change the **y** to **i** and add **ed**.

       hurry-hurried   try-tried

When the verb ends in a single consonant after a single short vowel, double the final consonant, then add **ed**.

       stop-stopped   knit-knitted

Make each of the following verbs show past tense.

1. study studied *Example*	1. name _____
2. bake _____	2. spy _____
3. smell _____	3. melt _____
4. wash _____	4. clip _____
5. smile _____	5. toast _____
6. grab _____	6. pop _____
7. copy _____	7. empty _____
8. trim _____	8. play _____

Past Tense Verbs

To make most verbs tell about the past, add **ed** to the basic form.

> cook-cook**ed**   clean-clean**ed**

When the verb ends in a silent **e**, drop the **e** and add **ed**.

> rak**e**-rak**ed**   hop**e**-hop**ed**

When the verb ends in **y** after a consonant, change the **y** to **i** and add **ed**.

> bur**y**-bur**ied**   sp**y**-sp**ied**

When the verb ends in a single consonant after a single short vowel, double the final consonant and add **ed**.

> clip-clip**ped**   pop-pop**ped**

Write each of the following verbs using the correct **ed** ending.

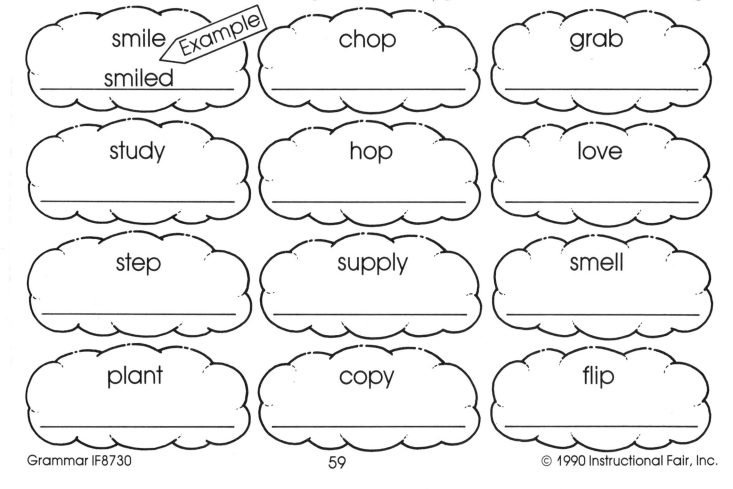

smile — Example
_____ smiled _____

chop
_____

grab
_____

study
_____

hop
_____

love
_____

step
_____

supply
_____

smell
_____

plant
_____

copy
_____

flip
_____

Past Tense With Helping Verbs

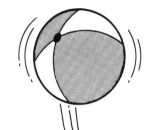

Helping verbs can be used to tell about the past. Use **has** with a singular subject.

She has kicked the ball.

Use **have** with a plural subject or with I or you.

The **boys have** kicked the ball.

Use **had** with a singular or plural subject.

I had kicked the ball.   **They had** kicked the ball.

Write sentences with the following verbs using a helping verb and the correct **ed** ending. Use only **has** or **have**.

stare	We have stared all day long. ◁ Example
bake	_____
worry	_____
jump	_____
arrive	_____
fix	_____
reply	_____
step	_____
change	_____
try	_____
brag	_____
close	_____
open	_____
ski	_____

Irregular Verbs

Some verbs change their basic form to show past tense.

eat-ate   do-did

Some of these verbs change their basic form again to show past tense with a helping verb.

eat-ate-has eaten   do-did-has done

Below are some irregular verbs you often use.

present	past alone	past with a helping verb
1. do	did	done
2. eat	ate	eaten
3. give	gave	given
4. go	went	gone
5. see	saw	seen
6. take	took	taken

In the sentences below, circle the correct form of the verb.

Example⟩ He has (did, done) his report.

1. Danny (ate, eaten) a pizza for lunch.

2. The photographer (took, taken) my picture.

3. They (went, gone) to Disneyland.

4. We have (saw, seen) the Statue of Liberty.

5. Gina was (gave, given) first prize.

6. My parents have (went, gone) to Detroit.

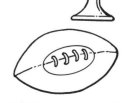

7. We (saw, seen) the greatest football game.

8. The class (took, taken) a field trip.

Irregular Verbs

Verbs that show past time in different ways are called irregular verbs.

Below are seven irregular verbs frequently used.

Present	Past-alone	Past with helping verb
break	broke	broken
bring	brought	brought
come	came	come
drive	drove	driven
do	did	done
eat	ate	eaten
give	gave	given

In the sentences below, circle the correct form of the verb.

Example > I have (did, (done)) the dishes.

1. We (ate, eaten) all the birthday cake.
2. Julie (came, come) to my piano recital.
3. Dad has (gave, given) me my allowance.
4. Mom (drove, driven) me to my soccer game.
5. Last night I (did, done) my homework.
6. My sister has (came, come) home from college.
7. My TV has been (broke, broken) a week.
8. Jimmy has (drove, driven) to Los Angeles.
9. Craig had (ate, eaten) too much ice cream.
10. I (broke, broken) my arm skiing in Colorado.
11. Elizabeth (did, done) me a big favor.
12. We have (gave, given) the problem much thought.
13. The Jordans (gave, give) a donation to the Red Cross.

Irregular Verbs

Below are seven more irregular verbs frequently used.

Present	Past-alone	Past with helping verb
grow	grew	grown
go	went	gone
run	ran	run
see	saw	seen
take	took	taken
throw	threw	thrown
write	wrote	written

In the sentences below, circle the correct form of the verb.

Example > Gavin has (grew, (grown)) two inches.

1. Our gym class (ran, run) the 50-yard dash.

2. My car should have (went, gone) to the repair shop.

3. Angela (saw, seen) the magic show.

4. Colin (threw, thrown) a snowball at Michael.

5. We have (ran, run) out of sugar.

6. Sharon has (wrote, written) a letter to Kathy.

7. We (took, taken) four rolls of film in Mexico.

8. We have (saw, seen) the Super Bowl.

9. After it rained, my flowers (grew, grown).

10. We (went, gone) on a cruise last July.

11. Have you (took, taken) out the trash?

12. I was (threw, thrown) off my horse.

13. Has the sick child (threw, thrown) up yet?

14. We had (went, gone) to Italy when it happened.

Name_____

Past Tense Verbs
Review

Write the correct spelling for each verb in the clouds so it will show past tense.

taste _Example_	fry	fix
tasted	_____	_____

knot	end	vote
_____	_____	_____

raise	stop	rub
_____	_____	_____

In the sentences below, circle the correct form of the verb.

Example ▷ I (did, done) my homework.

1. You have (ate, eaten) too many cookies.

2. Donna had (saw, seen) the ice show.

3. We (took, taken) flowers to grandma.

4. Our family (went, gone) to the beach.

5. Josh should have (did, done) the dishes.

6. Have you been (gave, given) the assignment?

7. We (ate, eaten) popcorn at the movie.

8. Mother had (took, taken) Jeff to the dentist.

9. After it rained, we (saw, seen) a rainbow.

10. Dad had (went, gone) on a business trip.

Pronouns

Name _____

Pronouns are words that stand for singular or plural nouns.

Helpful Hints	singular	plural
pronouns used to talk about yourself	I, me	we, us
pronouns used to talk to the person	you	you
pronouns used to talk about other persons or things	he, him, it, she, her	they, them

Copy the pronoun from each sentence into the party favor next to the sentence.

Example> He is my only brother.

1. Nancy had her teeth cleaned.

2. Is mother going with us?

3. Do you like chocolate pie?

4. Tommy is taking him a present.

5. They watched the football game.

6. Dad gave them some money.

7. I watched cartoons on TV.

8. We went fishing yesterday.

9. Kathy gave me a present.

10. He bought a new game.

Pronouns

subject

| I | HE | WE | SHE |

ME | US | HER | HIM | THEM

Not subject

A pronoun is used in place of a noun.
If the pronoun is the subject, use **I, we, he, she**.

Craig plays the violin.   Mindy plays the piano.
He plays the violin.   She plays the piano.

If the pronoun is not the subject, use **me, us, her, him, them.**

Mother took Connie shopping.   Dad went fishing with Alex.
Mother took her shopping.   Dad went fishing with him.

Use **it** and _____ t of a sentence.

Antecedents

Th_____ :   I waited for the bus.
                     I waited for it.

In the sentences below, choose the correct pronoun and write
it on the line after the senten___.

| Example > Karen _____ ent camping. | she _____ |

1. Danny and _____ng.   1. _____
2. (We, Us) went _____ game.   2. _____
3. The teacher too_____ to the library.   3. _____
4. (Him, He) was a ___nous American.   4. _____
5. Aunt Mary gave $1.00 to (them, we).   5. _____
6. (Her, You) and Greg are my best friends.   6. _____
7. Please take this note to (he, him).   7. _____
8. Charlie took Alan and (me, I) to the party.   8. _____
9. The teacher told (she, her) to talk louder.   9. _____
10. You and (he, him) gave a good report.   10. _____

66

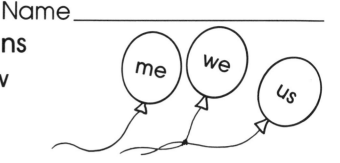

Pronouns
Review

In the following sentences, underline the pronouns. Write the noun or nouns the pronouns stand for on the blackboard below.

Example> Mary wore a blue dress. She spotted her dress.

1. The children played baseball. They won 6 to 2.
2. John and Tim raked leaves. Mother thanked them.
3. The dog ran in the street. Sally ran after him.
4. The boys saw a movie. It was scary.
5. The girls picked apples. Mother baked pies with them.
6. Freddy, would you please clean your room?
7. Mindy bought some peaches and paid $1.25 for them.
8. "Read me a poem, please," said Robin.
9. Sunshine is good for plants. It helps them grow.
10. Our class went on a trip. We had a picnic lunch.

Mary < Example

1. _____   5. _____

2. _____   6. _____

3. _____   7. _____

4. _____   8. _____

9. _____

10. _____

Possessive Pronouns

Pronouns that show ownership are called possessive pronouns. Some are used with nouns.

his dog   **her** cat   **our** pets

Some possessive pronouns are used without nouns.

The dog is **mine**.   The cat is **hers**.

pronouns used with a noun			pronouns used without a noun		
my	his	their	mine	his	its
our	her		ours	hers	
your	its		yours	theirs	

Write a new sentence using a possessive pronoun in place of the underlined words.

Example > Is this coat <u>your coat</u>?
Is this coat yours? _____

1. This house is <u>Cliff's house</u>.

   _____

2. <u>Nancy's</u> friends came for dinner.

   _____

3. <u>Angela and Jane's</u> school is large.

   _____

4. That bicycle is <u>my bicycle</u>.

   _____

5. This game is <u>your game</u>.

   _____

6. Pancake is <u>Bill's dog</u>.

Possessive Pronouns

The possessive form of a pronoun does not use an apostrophe. These are the possessive forms of pronouns.

my, mine	our, ours
your, yours	you, yours
his, her, hers, its	their, theirs

The dog lost **its** tag.   The twins rode **their** bikes.

In the following sentences, write the possessive pronoun on the line. Follow the information in the parentheses.

Example ⟩ The bracelet is __mine__ .
(The bracelet belongs to me.)

1. Comb _____ hair.

   (The hair belongs to you.)

2. The baby took _____ bottle.

   (The bottle belongs to the baby.)

3. The books were _____ .

   (The books belonged to Jim.)

4. _____ fur was wet.

   (The fur belonged to the dog.)

5. The mailman brought _____ mail.

   (The mail belonged to us.)

6. _____ flowers are in bloom.

   (The flowers belong to me.)

7. The blue bicycle is _____ .

   (The bicycle belongs to you.)

8. _____ piano lesson is today.

   (The piano lesson is Jill's.)

9. _____ TV set is broken.

   (The TV belongs to us.)

That banana is yours.

This banana is mine.

69

Pronouns Review

Circle the pronouns in the following story. There are 24 pronouns.

A Scary Dream

"They are coming after us," Rhonda said to her brother, Scott. Believe me, Scott, I saw them with their funny-looking faces. The two of them had long, orange hair, and they had gigantic feet. I thought they could be from Mars because they spoke a funny language.

One of them glared at me with his strange-looking face. The other one looked like she had on her clothes from outer space.

Scott, you can't imagine my thoughts as I saw them coming after me with their weird looks and their weird clothes.

Finish this story. Use at least 6 different pronouns. Circle the pronouns you use.

_____

_____

_____

_____

_____

_____

_____

_____

Name_____

Adjectives

An adjective is a word that describes a noun.

Adjectives ⟩ tell what kind
tell how many
tell which ones

bright sun
two birds
this tree

Complete each sentence below with an adjective that would describe each picture.

 Example

This shelf had

_four_____ books.

This is a _____ bus.

_____ bike is mine.

This is a _____ rose.

Look at the _____ kites.

This person is a _____ person.

This camel has _____ humps.

This looks like a _____ hamburger.

This tree has _____ leaves.

This _____ clown was in the circus.

This car has a _____ dent.

This dog has a _____ nose.

this
one
shiny   key
silver
that

Adjectives

fish

four
gold
pretty
small
these

An adjective is a word that describes a noun or pronoun.

Adjectives...

- tell **what kind.**   kitchen table   card table
- tell **how many.**   seven pencils   many pencils
- tell **which ones.**   this   that   these   those

In the following sentences, write an adjective on each line. Do not use an adjective more than one time. Answers will vary.

Example > My ___older___ brother has a ___blue___ bicycle.

1. My _____ skirt is plaid.

2. My _____ friend has _____ eyes.

3. The _____ weather was good for our garden.

4. _____ hat keeps my head warm.

5. The campers put up _____ tents.

6. Ben went to a _____ movie.

7. Mother picked up our _____ toys and _____ clothes.

8. We made a _____ , _____ vase in art class.

9. Dad is a _____ tennis player.

10. We saw _____ bears and _____ monkeys at the zoo.

11. Holly used her _____ calculator.

12. Our _____ dog is a _____ pet.

13. That _____ building is very _____ .

14. Sarah just got a _____ car and a _____ dog.

15. The _____ , _____ music drove my mom crazy.

Adjectives

Name _____

Write five adjectives that could describe the picture in the center of each flower. Do not use an adjective more than one time.

Answers will vary.

good ← Example

73   © 1990 Instructional Fair, Inc.

Name ____________________

Adjectives

Write three adjectives that describe each noun shown below. Do not use an adjective more than once.

book 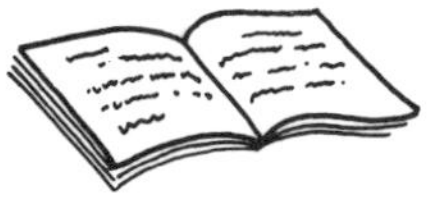 Example: long, good, true	feet 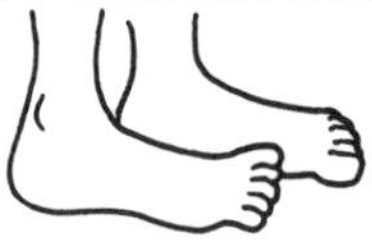	house 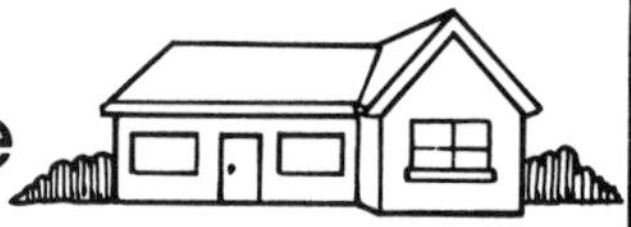
airplane 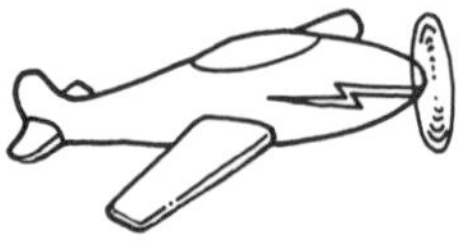	hot dog 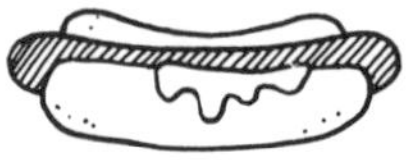	cloud 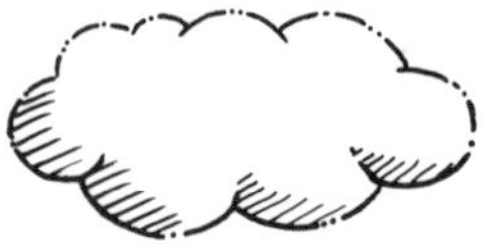
butterflies 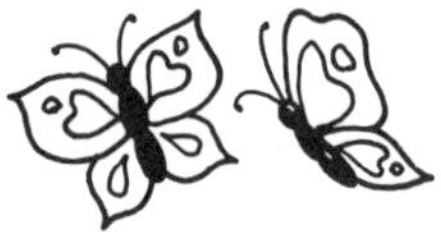	shoes 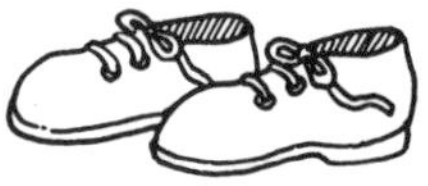	bells 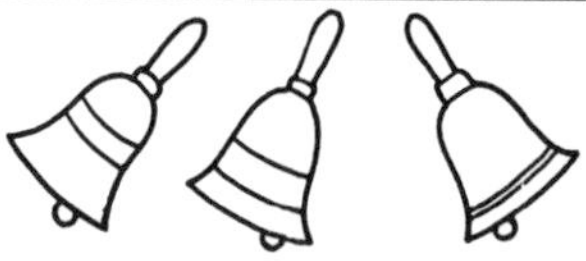
clown 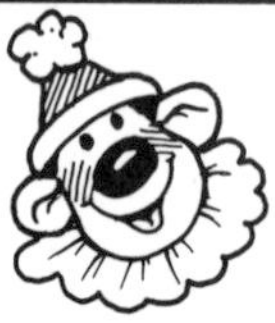	flowers 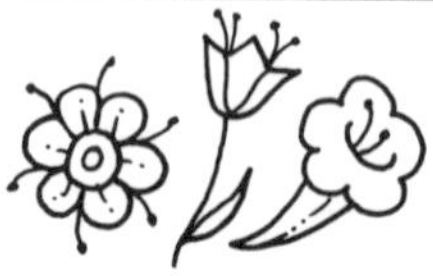	ice cream cone 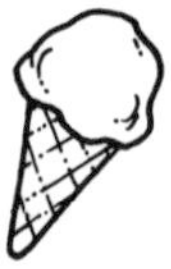

fluffy cloud

Adjectives

rain cloud

Fill in the blanks with an adjective. Be creative.

1. The _____ clouds in the _____ sky were

   _____ and _____ ones.

2. In the _____ morning, the _____

   children went to the _____ beach.

3. The _____ smell of the _____ pizza

   made the _____ children happy.

4. One _____ , _____ afternoon, my

   _____ friends and I went to a _____

   cave in the _____ woods near my

   _____ house.

5. The _____ creatures on the _____

   planet looked like _____ _____ men.

6. The _____ animals in the _____ zoo

   were _____ and _____ looking.

7. _____ children in our _____ class

   saw the _____ movie about the

   _____ people from the _____ Ages.

75

Nouns   Adjectives
Review

Underline the adjective in each sentence. Circle the noun it describes. Write the adjective and the noun it describes on the lines after the sentence.

	adjective	noun
Example > Kevin's (bike) is <u>blue</u>.	blue	bike
1. Billy likes hot cocoa.	_____	_____
2. Mr. Atkins ran in two marathons.	_____	_____
3. These cookies got burned.	_____	_____
4. We peeled many apples.	_____	_____
5. Tina has brown eyes.	_____	_____
6. We looked around the ugly room.	_____	_____
7. They ate fried chicken.	_____	_____
8. Molly prefers pumpkin pie.	_____	_____
9. I painted with water colors.	_____	_____
10. Ellen went to a surprise party.	_____	_____
11. Patrick read mystery books.	_____	_____
12. Take this package home.	_____	_____
13. We went in a new airplane.	_____	_____
14. Beth is very pretty.	_____	_____
15. We went to buy new clothes.	_____	_____

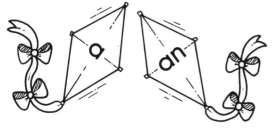

Name_____

Articles
"A"   "An"

Use **a** before words beginning with consonants.

a bird   a blue bird

Use **an** before words beginning with vowels.

an apple   an orange

Only use **a** or **an** before singular nouns.

a cow   an animal

Fill in each ☐ with **a** or **an**.

Example ⟩ Susie chose ⟨a⟩ piece of apple pie.

1. I have ☐ aunt named Mary.
2. We went to ☐ movie last night.
3. Mark wrote ☐ long letter.
4. We took ☐ English test.
5. Ned has ☐ old bicycle.
6. We had ☐ ice cream cone.
7. Maggie ate ☐ orange for breakfast.
8. They saw ☐ deer on their trip.
9. Steve thought the car was ☐ ugly color.
10. Emily bought ☐ new pair of skates.
11. He was ☐ officer in the army.
12. We built ☐ campfire.
13. ☐ elephant is such a large animal.
14. The group went to ☐ interesting museum.

On the back of this paper, write 3 sentences using **a** correctly and 3 sentences using **an** correctly.

a king

an ace

Articles

"A" and "An"

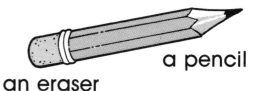

an eraser   a pencil

Use **A** before words beginning with consonant sounds.

a boy   a girl   a cat   a dog

Use **An** before words beginning with vowel sounds.

an apple   an onion   an Indian

Use **An** before words beginning with a silent **H**.

an hour   an honest friend

In the sentences below, circle the correct word.

Example > We saw (a, an) bird's nest.

a nest

1. Mark has (a, an) orange and brown sweater.
2. Two quarters equal (a, an) half dollar.
3. (A, An) engine pulled (a, an) long train.
4. They put up (a, an) target in the field.
5. There is (a, an) enormous house on (a, an) hill.
6. My family went to (a, an) opera in New York.
7. We talked to (a, an) teacher about (a, an) answer.
8. Meg had (a, an) art lesson after school.
9. I got (a, an) infield hit in the big game!
10. (A, An) exit sign hung over (a, an) door.
11. We had (a, an) aunt and (a, an) uncle for dinner.
12. We had (a, an) cookie and (a, an) ice cream cone.
13. Vince ran for (a, an) hour on (a, an) cinder track.
14. Jim learned (a, an) Indian dance on (a, an) reservation.
15. (A, An) honest friend is someone to treasure.

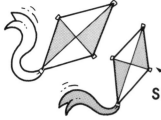

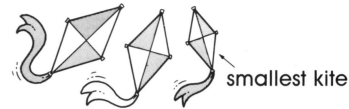

Adjectives

smaller kite   smallest kite

Add **er** to an adjective when you compare two people, places or things.

      smaller child   louder noise

Add **est** to an adjective when you compare three or more people, places or things.

      smallest child   loudest noise

In the sentences below, circle the correct form of the adjective in the parentheses.

Example > Gina was the ((older,) oldest) of the two girls.

1. Of the two towels, this one feels (softer, softest).
2. His story was the (longer, longest) one in his class.
3. Which of these two bananas is (smaller, smallest)?
4. The prices at Wong's store are the (lower, lowest) in town.
5. The kitchen is the (warmer, warmest) room in our house.
6. This cake is (sweeter, sweetest) than that pie.
7. Yesterday was the (colder, coldest) day we've had this winter.
8. Kenny is the (taller, tallest) of the twins.
9. My desk is the (neater, neatest) of the two.
10. Robin is the (smarter, smartest) of the children.
11. Let's watch the (shorter, shortest) movie on TV.
12. Which one of your parents is (older, oldest)?
13. Susan is the (prettier, prettiest) of the two girls.
14. The redwood is the (larger, largest) tree in the world.

Adjectives

big → bigger → biggest

Spelling Rules

When an adjective ends in a single consonant following a single vowel, double the final consonant and add **er** or **est**.

bigger   biggest

When an adjective ends in a silent **e**, drop the final **e** and add **er** or **est**.   wider   widest

If a word ends in **y**, following a consonant, change the **y** to **i** and add **er** or **est**.   sillier   silliest

Copy each adjective below. Then write the two forms it uses in comparison. Follow the spelling rules above.

Example ▷ **hot—**   hot,   hotter,   hottest

1. easy— _____ _____ _____

2. brave— _____ _____ _____

3. scary— _____ _____ _____

4. red— _____ _____ _____

5. nice— _____ _____ _____

6. hungry— _____ _____ _____

7. blue— _____ _____ _____

8. noisy— _____ _____ _____

9. flat— _____ _____ _____

10. fast— _____ _____ _____

On another piece of paper, write a sentence showing comparison for each of the following adjectives:

safer, safest   richer, richest   tighter, tightest
happier, happiest   bluer, bluest   riper, ripest

80

more delicious

most delicious

Adjectives
"More" and "Most"

Longer adjectives are usually compared by the use of **more** and **most**.

Use **more** to compare two people, places or things.
   Dale is **more helpful** than Pat.

Use **most** to compare three or more people, places or things.
   Holly was the **most helpful** student in the class.

If you use more or most, do not use **er** or **est**.
   right: This tree is **larger** than that one.
   wrong: This tree is **more larger** than that one.

In the sentences below, circle the correct form of the adjective in the parentheses.

Example > Jose seems (more happier, (happier)) than Juan.

1. This is the (more useful, most useful) book in the library.

2. Brand X keeps my clothes (cleaner, more cleaner) than Brand Y.

3. The movie was the (most scariest, scariest) I've ever seen.

4. Donna is the (more beautiful, most beautiful) of the twins.

5. Ricky is (more taller, taller) than his dad.

6. Of all the flavors, chocolate is the (more delicious, most delicious).

7. Nicky's joke was (funnier, more funnier) than mine.

8. Eileen's report was the (most neatest, neatest) one in her class.

9. That rose is the (more unusual, most unusual) one I have.

Adjectives

2nd. place

better

Name _____

good

best

A few adjectives change to completely new words when they are used to compare things. Two of these adjectives are the words **good** and **bad**.

    good—This is a **good** book.

    better—My book is **better** than your book.

    best—This is the **best** book I've ever read.

    bad—The weather is **bad** today.

    worse—The weather is **worse** today than yesterday.

    worst—Today's weather is the **worst** of the winter.

In the sentences below, circle the correct form of the adjective in the parentheses.

Example > Lunch today is (good, (better,) best) than yesterday.

1. This is the (bad, worse, worst) pizza I have ever eaten.

2. My shoes are in (bad, worse, worst) condition than yours.

3. My grades are the (good, better, best) in the class.

4. Mother has a (good, better, best) set of dishes.

5. This tool is the (good, better, best) one I have.

6. I wore my (bad, worse, worst) jeans to the picnic.

7. My brownies are (good, better, best) than yours.

8. This is a (bad, worse, worst) snowstorm.

9. This one looks even (good, better, best) than that one.

10. My brother's room looks (bad, worse, worst) than mine.

11. Your tennis shoes have the (good, better, best) soles.

12. This headache is the (bad, worse, worst) I've ever had.

Nouns
Adjectives
Review

big, beautiful rose

In the sentences below, underline the adjectives and circle the nouns they describe. Do not use **a** or **an**.

Example > My dog is young and frisky.

1. Dad bought a new blue car.
2. This winter has been cold and icy.
3. The furry cat hid under my back porch.
4. The brave firemen rescued the small children.
5. My parents bought a new table and lamp.
6. Many birds ate from our large birdhouse.
7. The American flag is red, white and blue.
8. Jeff has one brother and two sisters.
9. I needed a sharp knife to cut the tough meat.
10. The handsome man married the beautiful lady.
11. The mysterious spaceship landed in the dense forest.
12. Ten chocolate cupcakes were on the large plate.
13. The longest race of the day lasted one hour.

14. Your tennis shoes look newer than mine.
15. The young children walked along the sandy beach.
16. Ten clowns climbed out of the tiny car.
17. My dog chased the little, black kitten up a tree.
18. Susan made six bibs for her tiny nephew.
19. Many people attended the big race last Saturday.
20. The funniest act had the two crazy clowns.

Adverbs

An adverb answers the questions, **How?**, **When?** or **Where?** about verbs. Many adverbs end in **ly** when answering the question, **How?**

Our team won the game <u>easily</u>. **How?**

Circle the adverb in each sentence. In the book below, tell which question it answers.

Example > My birthday is(today.)

1. The children played quietly at home.

2. We went to the movie yesterday.

3. My friends are coming inside to play.

4. The child cut his meat carefully.

5. The girls went upstairs to get their coats.

6. The play-off games start tomorrow.

7. The boys walked slowly toward the bus.

8. The teacher said, "Write your name neatly."

9. We ate outside on a picnic table.

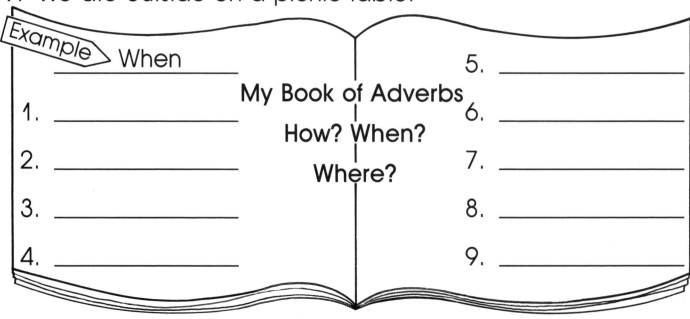

Example > When
_____

1. _____

2. _____

3. _____

4. _____

My Book of Adverbs

How? When?

Where?

5. _____

6. _____

7. _____

8. _____

9. _____

Adverbs

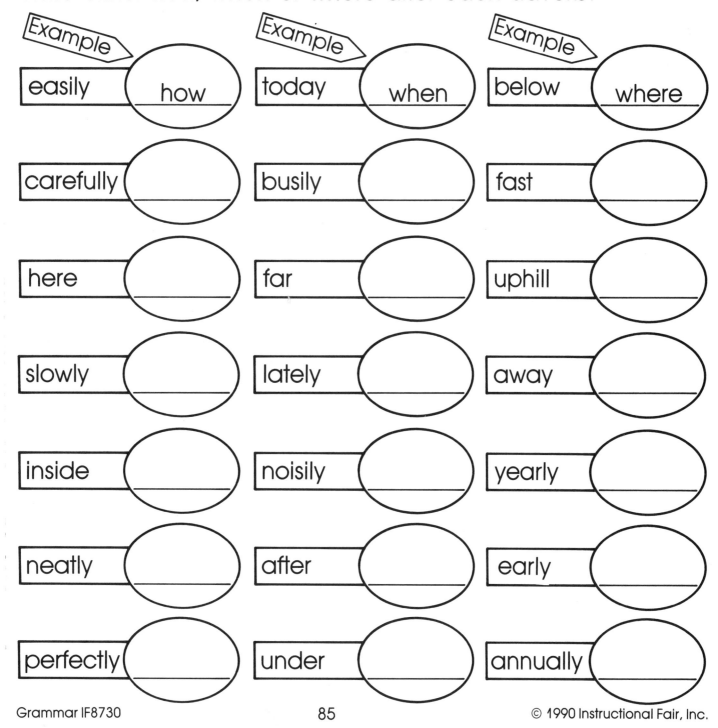

Name _____

Adverbs modify verbs or adjectives and tell **how**, **when** or **where**.

How—I read **slowly**.
Where—I read **inside**.
When—I was reading **today**.

How when where ??

Write either **how**, **when** or **where** after each adverb.

Example	Example	Example
easily — how	today — when	below — where
carefully —	busily —	fast —
here —	far —	uphill —
slowly —	lately —	away —
inside —	noisily —	yearly —
neatly —	after —	early —
perfectly —	under —	annually —

Grammar IF8730   85   © 1990 Instructional Fair, Inc.

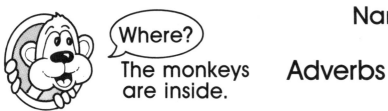

Where?

The monkeys are inside.

Adverbs

In the sentences below, write an adverb on the line to complete each sentence. The word in parentheses tells the kind of adverb to write. Do not use an adverb more than once. Answers will vary.

| Example ⟩ The car is _____here_____ . | (where) |

1. Our team played _____ . (when)

2. Brian writes _____ . (how)

3. The cows move _____ . (how)

4. Melissa will dance _____ . (when)

5. My dog went _____ . (where)

6. We ran _____ . (how)

7. The choir sang _____ . (how)

8. The cat purred _____ . (where)

9. Hilary spoke _____ . (how)

10. We'll go on our vacation _____ . (when)

11. The sign goes _____ . (where)

12. Mother brought the groceries _____ . (where)

13. David read the directions _____ . (how)

14. We'll be leaving _____ . (when)

15. We have three bedrooms _____ . (where)

16. Our family goes on a vacation _____ . (when)

17. Jim ran _____ down the street. (how)

18. They_____ laid the baby in the crib. (how)

19. The man went _____ with his paper. (where)

20. My dad gets a raise in pay_____ . (when)

Verbs
Adverbs

Review

In the sentences below, draw a line under every adverb and circle every verb. Write the verbs and adverbs in the proper column after each sentence.

	Verb	Adverb
Example > We did our chores quietly.	did	quietly
1. Jason got his bicycle early.	_____	_____
2. Slowly, I cleaned my room.	_____	_____
3. Lucy often rides her horse.	_____	_____
4. We walked cautiously on the ice.	_____	_____
5. I washed my car today.	_____	_____
6. Suddenly, it started to snow.	_____	_____
7. Derek took his wagon outside.	_____	_____
8. The child used the scissors carefully.	_____	_____
9. Jackie went home early.	_____	_____
10. Bill slid safely into second base.	_____	_____
11. Shari happily got 100% on her test.	_____	_____
12. My cousin came again to visit.	_____	_____
13. Earlier, I helped the principal.	_____	_____
14. The soldiers bravely fought.	_____	_____
15. We quickly finished the puzzle.	_____	_____
16. Yesterday, I baked brownies.	_____	_____
17. Susie takes her shower upstairs.	_____	_____
18. My dad gets his paycheck monthly.	_____	_____
19. The twins threw the toys everywhere.	_____	_____
20. The mouse crept out quietly.	_____	_____

Nouns-Pronouns
Adjectives
Verbs-Adverbs
Review

In the sentences below, label each of the following.

N—for noun **Adj** —for adjective
P —for pronoun **Adv**—for adverb
V —for verb

Adj Adj N V   Adv

Example > The little girl ran outside.

1. We feed the birds regularly.

2. Derek planted a maple tree yesterday.

3. Charles wrote them a letter.

4. They have two small dogs.

5. Rosie will be dancing tomorrow.

6. The toys were everywhere.

7. The three children are going swimming today.

8. You can eat now.

9. They washed the car carefully.

10. Several thirsty children drank cold lemonade.

11. We run three miles often.

12. The chorus has been singing beautifully.

13. He gave Chuck five dollars.

14. Pam washed the dishes slowly.

15. That tiny baby was sleeping soundly.

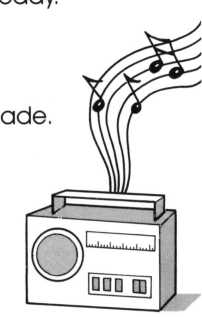

Contractions

Contractions are made by putting together two words. When the words are put together, at least one letter is left out. An apostrophe is used in place of the missing letters.

Below are some examples.

word + will	I will → I'll	
word + is	she is → she's	
word + has	he has → he's	
word + are	they are → they're	
word + have	they have → they've	
word + not	has not → hasn't	
word + would	he would → he'd	

has

hasn't

not

On the bulletin board below, write a contraction for the following words.

1. is not
2. she is
3. they have
4. he is

5. I would
6. you are
7. she will
8. did not

9. he will
10. where is
11. they would
12. she has

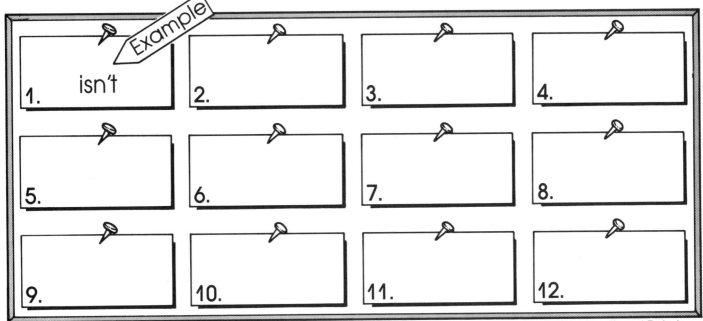

Example

1. isn't
2.
3.
4.

5.
6.
7.
8.

9.
10.
11.
12.

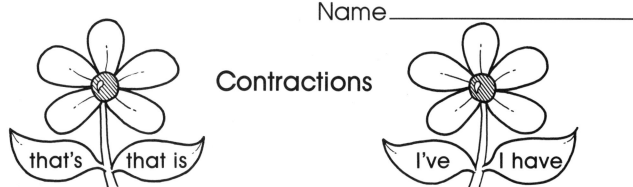

Contractions

Contractions are made by putting two words together. When the words are put together, at least one letter is left out. An apostrophe is used in place of the missing letters. Below are some examples. Notice the patterns.

word plus is	she is → she's	he is → he's
word plus will	I will → I'll	she will → she'll
word plus has	she has → she's	he has → he's
word plus are	they are → they're	we are → we're
word plus have	they have → they've	we have → we've
word plus not	has not → hasn't	did not → didn't
word plus would	he would → he'd	they would → they'd

Write a contraction for each of these words.

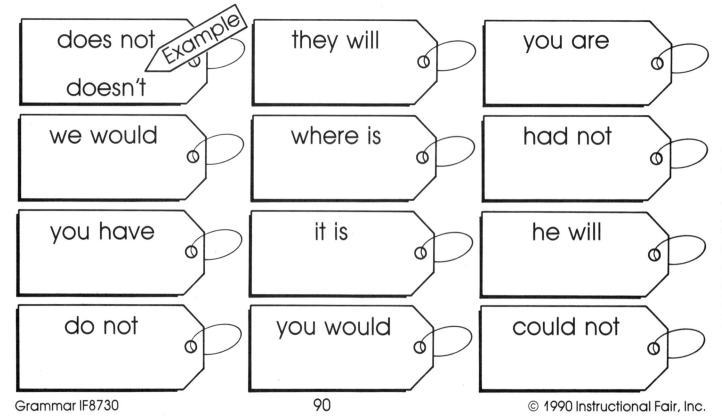

does not / Example / doesn't	they will	you are
we would	where is	had not
you have	it is	he will
do not	you would	could not

Contractions
Review

We're on our way.

Copy the following words. Add the apostrophe where it belongs.

1. Im   I'm ___ Example
2. hasnt _____
3. hed   _____
4. arent _____
5. shes   _____
6. well   _____

7. theres _____
8. wed   _____
9. Ill   _____
10. were   _____
11. youre _____
12. thats _____

Write the two words which form each of the following contractions.

1. weren't were not ___ Example
2. I've   _____
3. I'll   _____
4. wouldn't _____
5. here's   _____
6. they're _____

7. it's   _____
8. shouldn't _____
9. you'll   _____
10. I'd   _____
11. wasn't _____
12. you've _____

Contractions
Review

I'm going.

I'll go.

We'll go.

Copy the following words. Add an apostrophe where it belongs.

Example

cant can't	wed	Im	youre
theyll	were	didnt	well
couldnt	Ill	theyd	its

Write two words for each of the following contractions.

Example

we'll we will	isn't	I've	that's
shouldn't	aren't	weren't	there's
you'll	I'd	wasn't	you've

Name_____

Negative Words

Not words and No words are called negatives. Do not use a **not** word and a **no** word together in a sentence. **Never** is also a negative word.

Right: We never go to bed early.
Wrong: We don't never go to bed early.

Circle the correct word in the parentheses.

Example▷ We don't want (no, (any)) more dessert.

1. We weren't (never, ever) friends.

2. The music was so loud, we didn't hear (nothing, anything).

3. My dog won't hurt (anybody, nobody).

4. Our team hasn't scored (any, no) runs yet.

5. The child (has, hasn't) done nothing wrong.

6. I haven't (never, ever) used my new camera.

7. I didn't see (no, any) planes landing.

8. Bob (could, couldn't) never finish a large pizza.

9. My cousin hasn't gone (nowhere, anywhere).

10. You (should, shouldn't) never slam the door.

11. Connie, (are, aren't) you never going to finish this?

12. I (haven't, have) never been to England.

13. Judy (is, isn't) never on time for school.

14. There (was, wasn't) never enough snow to ski.

15. Steve didn't (never, ever) forget his mother's birthday.

Negative Words

The words **not**, **no** and **never** are negative words. You must avoid using two negative words in a sentence.

Right—There is no popcorn left.
Wrong—There isn't no popcorn left.

Circle the correct word in the parentheses.

Example ⟩ Michelle ((could) couldn't) run no faster.

1. I didn' (ever, never) wear braces.
2. My teacher hasn't (none, any) of our grades yet.
3. Kim couldn't drive (no one, anyone) home.
4. Isn't (anybody, nobody) going with me?
5. My family (hasn't, has) no time to travel this year.
6. I don't like to go (nowhere, anywhere) alone.
7. Chris (has, hasn't) done no homework.
8. We (wouldn't, would) never lie to you.
9. Why didn't I get (none, any)?
10. Andy hasn't (no, any) film for his camera.
11. Diana, (are, aren't) you never going to finish this?
12. Todd (wasn't, was) saving no money at all.
13. We aren't able to do (any, no) magic tricks.
14. Won't you (never, ever) return my record?

Write a sentence for each of the following words: never, nothing, don't, nobody.

_____

_____

_____

Name _____

Periods

On the lookout for periods.

Use a period...

- at the end of a statement or command.
    statement—I like to play games.
    command—Wash the dishes.
- after an initial.
    Franklin D. Roosevelt   C. J. Muggs
- after an abbreviation.
    in.–inch   Mon.–Monday   Ave.–Avenue

In the sentences below, use a period where needed.

Example > Dr. M. Jones is my doctor.

1. Megan ran one mi on Boise Dr yesterday

2. Mrs Kelly bought a gal of milk

3. Mr Harold B Long is my uncle

4. The Long Co is on McNair St and Second Ave

5. Andrew has a three ft ruler

6. Wed , Sept 3rd, will be my birthday

7. Lt George S Brown lost 15 lbs on his diet

8. Ms Howe baked a doz cupcakes

9. Waterman Blvd is very wide at Union Ave

10. Thurs , we will go to St Louis

11. The baby weighed 6 lbs 12 oz at birth

12. Tues , Gov R Hayes will take office

13. Feb is the month I lost 10 lbs on my diet

14. Wood Creations, Inc is on Main St and Jones Blvd

Commas

Entering
Atlanta, Georgia

Use a comma...

- between the day and the year in a date.
    November 17, 1955
- between a city and a state.
    Denver, Colorado
- in a series of three or more persons or things.
    apples, oranges and plums.*

In the sentences below, place commas where needed.

Example ⟩ Matthew was born August 7, 1978.

1. Kara Sue and Patti played together.

2. On May 12 1980 we moved to Dallas Texas.

3. The Statue of Liberty is in New York City New York.

4. Grandma and Grandpa were married June 12 1942.

5. Mia has roses pansies and daisies in her garden.

6. The American flag is red white and blue.

7. I moved from Miami Florida to Cleveland Ohio.

8. Hawaii became a state August 21 1959.

9. Tommy Gary Adam and Jerry are my best friends.

10. On Monday Tuesday and Wednesday it snowed.

11. John F. Kennedy was shot November 22 1963.

12. We drive through Chicago Illinois on our way to Madison Wisconsin.

*Some textbooks place a comma before the and.
    apples, oranges, and plums

Commas

Use a comma...

- after the greeting and closing in a friendly letter.
  Dear Nina,   Yours truly, Jason

- to set off a direct quotation from the rest of the sentence.
  Andy said, "Meet me at 7:00."

- after yes or no at the beginning of a sentence or after the name of a person spoken to.
  Yes, I'm feeling better.   Amy, how do you feel?

In the sentences below, use a comma where needed.

Example> Terry, what is your dog's name?

1. Christine asked "How old are you?"

2. Mother said "I'm going to work."

3. Yes I have finished the dishes.

4. Nicky what T.V. program are you watching?

5. No I have not finished my homework.

6. Lorna where did you go on your vacation?

In the letter below, use commas where needed.

Dear Rachel

Did you go to Seattle Washington last summer? I went to visit my cousins in Detroit Michigan. When I got home Mom said "Debbie did you have fun?"

I said "Yes it was great."

Rachel I hope to see you soon.

Your friend

Debbie

Commas

A comma is used...

- to separate the day of the month from the year.   May 3, 1976
- to separate a city from a state or country.   Dallas, Texas
- to set off the name of a person spoken to.   Brad, come here.
- after yes or no at the beginning of a sentence.
     Yes, I can come.
- to set words apart in a series.* I like apples, grapes and pears,
- after the first complete thought in a sentence with two
     thoughts.   Hurry up, or we'll be late.
- after the greeting of a friendly letter and after the closing of
     every letter.   Dear Anita,   Sincerely, Dan
- to set off a direct quotation.   'I'm coming," said Al.

In the following sentences, use commas where they are
needed.

Example > Teddy, did you go to Utah, Nevada and Colorado?

1. My parents were married March 24 1967.

2. After swimming skating is my favorite sport.

3. I signed my letter Yours truly Tracy.

4. "Patti I'll be home late " said mother.

5. On December 6 1981 Carlos came to America.

6. Exams will be Tuesday Wednesday and Thursday.

7. Sarah missed the bus so she had to walk home.

8. I took my notebook to class but I forgot my pencil.

9. Tim asked "Is that a good book?"

10. On the way home I ran into a fence.

11. Yes I bought cereal milk bread and tuna.

12. We went from Miami Florida to Tulsa Oklahoma.

*Some textbooks teach that a comma is required before
   the "and".

Apostrophes

Use an apostrophe...

- in possessive nouns.
    singular–Teddy's record   Sharon's game
    plural–men's club   bears' tracks

- in contractions.
    I am–I'm   did not–didn't

In the groups of words below, make the underlined word show possession by using an apostrophe.

Example▷ <u>Kevins</u> baseball.   <u>Kevin's</u>

1. the <u>firemens</u> boots   1. _____

2. three <u>trains</u> tracks   2. _____

3. a <u>ships</u> decks   3. _____

4. <u>Lynns</u> house   4. _____

5. several <u>friends</u> games   5. _____

6. many <u>players</u> uniforms   6. _____

Write the contraction of these words by using an apostrophe.

Example▷ could not <u>couldn't</u>

1. he will _____   5. were not _____

2. you are _____   6. we have _____

3. he is _____   7. they are _____

4. It is _____   8. she will _____

Quotation Marks

Have you read, "Where the River Begins"?

Use quotation marks...

- to set off a direct quotation.
    The teacher said, "Kate, you got 100% on your test."

- around titles of poems, stories and reports.
    Todd read, "The Owl and The Pussycat."

Quotation marks are placed after the period or question mark.

In the sentences below, place quotation marks where needed.

Example> "Turn off the lights," Mother said.

1. Mr. Gordon asked, Daniel, are you going with me?

2. Grandma read me the story, The Rat in the Hat.

3. Miracle on 34th Street is one of my favorite movies.

4. Are you going to the play? Millie asked.

5. Anna gave a report called, Indians of the Southwest.

6. My brother can read, Spot Goes to School.

7. Luke remarked, It's very cold today.

8. Gavin read a report titled, Inside the Personal Computer.

9. Let's get together tomorrow, said Diana.

10. Have you read the poem called, Dancers Delight?

11. Joey said, Dave, let's play after school.

12. Jenny's report was titled, Great Painters.

Name _____

Quotation Marks
Apostrophes

Use quotation marks...

• before and after the words of every direct quotation.

    Margie asked, "What's for lunch?"

• around titles of stories, song titles, poems and reports.

    I read the poem, "Rip Van Winkle."

Use an apostrophe...

• to show where letters have been left out of contractions.

    they'll   we're   wouldn't

• to show ownership or possession.

    Donna's shoes   hikers' boots

In the following sentences, use quotation marks and apostrophes where they are needed.

Example ▷ Wasn't "The Rose and the Key" a good story?

1. The players equipment was kept in their lockers.
2. I ve finished my report, Famous Athletes.
3. Jennifer replied, I d love to come to your party.
4. My poem, The Beautiful Butterfly, won first prize.
5. Robbie s hamsters are frisky.
6. It s Ginny s coat that Sandy is wearing.
7. Aren t the boys bikes in the garage?
8. We re doing our report on rockets together.
9. The reporters stories were all too long.
10. My friend s birthday is tomorrow.
11. How to Handle Snakes, was the title of my report.
12. My sister s favorite album is Michael Jackson s Thriller.

Punctuation Marks Review

In the sentences below, place periods, commas, apostrophes and quotation marks where needed.

Example > "Yes, I'm going to the movie," said Ian.

1. Our family lives in Memphis Tennessee

2. The boys bicycles were new

3. I ve an uncle named T R Mayberry

4. Mrs Jordan Lori and Bonnie went to the fair

5. Aunt Helen said I ll be home late tonight

6. Didn t you measure 5 ft last year

7. Willy asked How much is the candy

8. Mother read us The Very Busy Spider

9. I m going to buy books erasers and pencils

10. Gail were you born Dec 14 1975

11. They re reading The Ships Voyage

12. Sandy please buy a lb of apples

13. Holly said Mom and Dad were married May 2 1955

14. Shouldn t we read Travel the U S A

15. We re going to Dr Gibbon s office

16. The three boys sweaters were left in Reid Ohio

17. Ebb Tide is Josephs favorite old song

18. Mr Evans were you in Dallas Texas on May 1 1985

19. Who s going to read the main character s part

20. Vince asked Where s the cars lights

Answer Key

Page 1

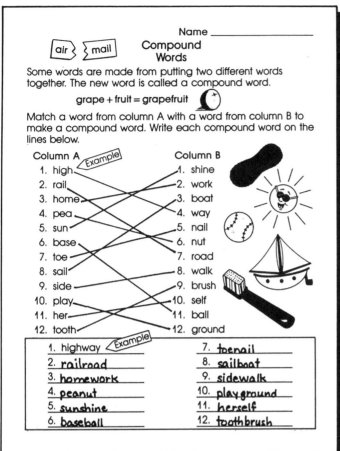

Name _____

Compound Words

Some words are made from putting two different words together. The new word is called a compound word.

grape + fruit = grapefruit

Match a word from column A with a word from column B to make a compound word. Write each compound word on the lines below.

Column A (Example)

1. high
2. rail
3. home
4. pea
5. sun
6. base
7. toe
8. sail
9. side
10. play
11. her
12. tooth

Column B

1. shine
2. work
3. boat
4. way
5. nail
6. nut
7. road
8. walk
9. brush
10. self
11. ball
12. ground

1. highway (Example)
2. railroad
3. homework
4. peanut
5. sunshine
6. baseball
7. toenail
8. sailboat
9. sidewalk
10. playground
11. herself
12. toothbrush

Page 2

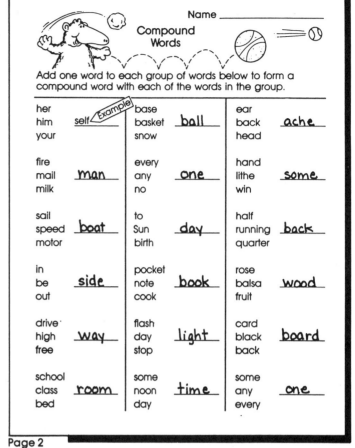

Name _____

Compound Words

Add one word to each group of words below to form a compound word with each of the words in the group.

her / him / your	self (Example)	base / basket / snow	ball	ear / back / head	ache
fire / mail / milk	man	every / any / no	one	hand / lithe / win	some
sail / speed / motor	boat	to / Sun / birth	day	half / running / quarter	back
in / be / out	side	pocket / note / cook	book	rose / balsa / fruit	wood
drive / high / free	way	flash / day / stop	light	card / black / back	board
school / class / bed	room	some / noon / day	time	some / any / every	one

Page 3

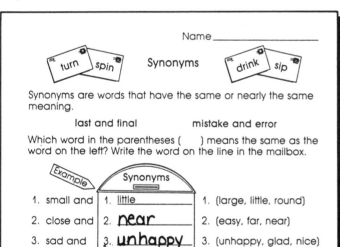

Name _____

Synonyms

Synonyms are words that have the same or nearly the same meaning.

last and final   mistake and error

Which word in the parentheses ( ) means the same as the word on the left? Write the word on the line in the mailbox.

Example

Synonyms

1. small and | 1. little | 1. (large, little, round)
2. close and | 2. near | 2. (easy, far, near)
3. sad and | 3. unhappy | 3. (unhappy, glad, nice)
4. bright and | 4. brilliant | 4. (dull, brilliant, clean)
5. false and | 5. wrong | 5. (clear, true, wrong)
6. large and | 6. huge | 6. (little, lamp, huge)
7. gift and | 7. present | 7. (give, present, store)
8. fast and | 8. quick | 8. (fresh, tame, quick)
9. tidy and | 9. neat | 9. (neat, seed, near)
10. stone and | 10. rock | 10. (store, rock, circle)
11. fat and | 11. plump | 11. (tall, square, plump)
12. raise and | 12. lift | 12. (lower, lift, carry)

Page 4

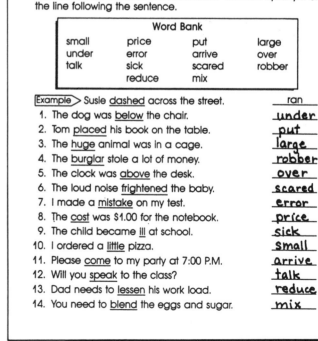

Name _____

Synonyms

Synonyms are words that have the same or nearly the same meaning.

Select a synonym for the underlined word in the sentences below from the words in The Word Bank. Write the synonym on the line following the sentence.

Word Bank

small	price	put	large
under	error	arrive	over
talk	sick	scared	robber
	reduce	mix	

Example > Susie dashed across the street. — ran

1. The dog was below the chair. — under
2. Tom placed his book on the table. — put
3. The huge animal was in a cage. — large
4. The burglar stole a lot of money. — robber
5. The clock was above the desk. — over
6. The loud noise frightened the baby. — scared
7. I made a mistake on my test. — error
8. The cost was $1.00 for the notebook. — price
9. The child became ill at school. — sick
10. I ordered a little pizza. — small
11. Please come to my party at 7:00 P.M. — arrive
12. Will you speak to the class? — talk
13. Dad needs to lessen his work load. — reduce
14. You need to blend the eggs and sugar. — mix

Answer Key

Page 5

Name _____

Antonyms

Antonyms are words that have opposite meanings.

Select an antonym for the underlined words in the sentences below from the words in the Word Bank. Write the antonym on the line following each sentence.

Word Bank

unbolt	strong	purchase	cooked
sharp	evil	ancient	assemble
minor	present	praised	learned
disarray	increase	day	

Example > The salesperson was <u>courteous</u>. — rude

1. The old man was <u>feeble</u>. — **strong**
2. The castle was <u>modern</u> inside. — **ancient**
3. Caroline likes <u>raw</u> carrots. — **cooked**
4. The character in the book was <u>good</u>. — **evil**
5. She <u>taught</u> Spanish every day. — **learned**
6. Doug was <u>absent</u> yesterday. — **present**
7. The knife was <u>dull</u> and rusty. — **sharp**
8. The teacher <u>criticized</u> the student. — **praised**
9. <u>Lock</u> the door, please. — **unbolt**
10. The meeting will <u>adjourn</u> soon. — **assemble**
11. It was a <u>major</u> decision. — **minor**
12. I am going to <u>sell</u> shoes. — **purchase**
13. You should <u>decrease</u> your sugar intake. — **Increase**
14. We went fishing in the middle of the <u>night</u>. — **day**
15. The room was in great <u>order</u>. — **disarray**

Page 5

Page 6

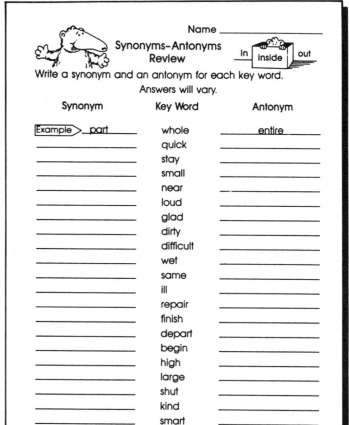

Name _____

Synonyms-Antonyms Review

Write a synonym and an antonym for each key word.

Answers will vary.

Synonym	Key Word	Antonym
Example > part	whole	entire
	quick	
	stay	
	small	
	near	
	loud	
	glad	
	dirty	
	difficult	
	wet	
	same	
	ill	
	repair	
	finish	
	depart	
	begin	
	high	
	large	
	shut	
	kind	
	smart	

Page 6

Page 7

Name _____

Homonyms

Words that are pronounced the same, but their meanings and their spellings are not the same, are called homonyms.

Read the homonyms in the parentheses ( ). Write one of the homonyms in a blank in each sentence.

Example > (two-to)
We have ___two___ apples.
We went ___to___ the store.

(pear-pair-pare)
I ate the delicious **pear**.
I have a **pair** of gloves.
Will you **pare** the peaches?

(sun-son)
They have a **son** and a daughter.
The **sun** is shining today.

(ate-eight)
I **ate** a pizza for lunch.
I bought **eight** pencils.

(red-read)
I **read** the book.
My book is **red**.

(one-won)
I **won** the race.
I have **one** brother.

Page 7

Page 8

Name _____

Homonyms

The sail is blue.
~~sale~~ ~~blew~~

Homonyms are words that sound the same, but have different spellings and meanings.

In the sentences below, circle the correct word.

Example > We used (flower, (flour)) in our cake.

1. We went ((to) too, two) the store.
2. The pig's (tale, (tail)) was short.
3. The ((knight) night) rode a beautiful horse.
4. I have a (soar, (sore)) on my knee.
5. Mother said, "Please do not ((waste) waist) time."
6. We had rare ((steak) stake) for dinner.
7. We can (beet, (beat)) your team playing baseball.
8. Did you (rap, (wrap)) the present?
9. Do not run down the ((stairs) stares).
10. Let's (paws, (pause)) for a drink of water.
11. Are you going to ((wait) weight) for me?
12. I'm taking a ((course) coarse) in English.
13. Have you (scene, (seen)) my science book?
14. The ((sum) some) of the problem is 10.
15. Which soda did you (chews, (choose))?
16. May I have a ((piece) peace) of cake?
17. I have sand in my (pale, (pail)).
18. Please come to (hour, (our)) house.
19. My ((aunt) ant) and uncle took us to the zoo.
20. Did you tie a square (not, (knot))?

Page 8

Answer Key

Homonyms

Our tents ✓
Hour tense

There are four homonyms in each of the silly sentences. Rewrite each sentence using the correct words.

Example >
The bare eight for pairs.
The bear ate four pears.

1. I wood like the hole piece of stake.
   I would like the whole piece of steak.
2. Isle where my blew genes tomorrow.
   I'll wear my blue jeans tomorrow.
3. Hour male is knot do today.
   Our mail is not due today.
4. Last knight we one for sense.
   Last night we won four cents.
5. Inn to daze we go on our crews.
   In two days we go on our cruise.
6. Next weak my ant mite come hear.
   Next week my aunt might come here.
7. My sun will by knew close.
   My son will buy new clothes.
8. The plain witch flu bye was noisy.
   The plane which flew by was noisy.
9. Ewe weight write near the gait.
   You wait right near the gate.
10. Eye sea my deer friend nose you.
    I see my dear friend knows you.

Page 9

Prefixes

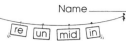
re un mid in

New words may be made from other words. One way to build a new word is to add a part to the beginning of a word.

Part	+	word	=	new word	
re	+	place	=	replace	(do again)
un	+	even	=	uneven	(not)
mid	+	air	=	midair	(middle)
in	+	different	=	indifferent	(not)

Use one of the above prefixes to write a new word that means the same as the description below.

Example > in the middle of summer   midsummer

1. paint again   **repaint**
2. not fair   **unfair**
3. not complete   **incomplete**
4. mount again   **remount**
5. not touched   **untouched**
6. wind again   **rewind**
7. not clear   **unclear**
8. do again   **redo**
9. not direct   **indirect**
10. not fit   **unfit**
11. in the middle of the day   **midday**

Page 10

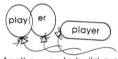
play er
player

Suffixes

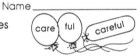
care ful
careful

Another way to build a new word is to add a part at the end of the word.

word	+	part	=	new word	(a person or thing who does something)
sing	+	er	=	singer	
care	+	less	=	careless	(without)
skill	+	ful	=	skillful	(full of)

Use one of the above suffixes to write a new word for the underlined word that means the same as the description.

Example > one who can jump   jumper

1. full of wonder   **wonderful**
2. without hope   **hopeless**
3. full of grace   **graceful**
4. without worth   **worthless**
5. one who can clean   **cleaner**
6. full of success   **successful**
7. without use   **useless**
8. one who can read   **reader**
9. without help   **helpless**
10. one who can teach **teacher**
11. full of cheer   **cheerful**

Page 11

Prefixes Suffixes Review

In each sentence below, find a word with a prefix or a suffix. Circle the root word. Draw a line under the prefix or the suffix.

Example > The dentist said it would be (pain)less.
Example > My washing machine has a (pre)soak) cycle.

1. Every sentence should be (meaning)ful.
2. Do not be (care)less about your clothes.
3. I need to re(do) my report.
4. The grizzly bear gave a (fright)ful roar.
5. My mis(fortune) was breaking my arm.
6. The (garden)er began planting seeds in May.
7. The recipe said to pre(cook) the meat.
8. Did you un(lock) your suitcase?
9. In our city, the weather is (change)able.
10. Wendy started pre(school) last September.
11. Andrew has a collection of (wood)en soldiers.
12. We live mid(way) between New York and Boston.
13. My grandparents are in(active).
14. The (paint)er needed a ladder for the ceiling.
15. Make the check (pay)able to Dr. Weaver.
16. My new kitchen chairs are un(comfortable).
17. The table had a (wash)able surface.
18. I think I'm pre(destined) to be a teacher.
19. That newspaper (reporter) seems hotheaded!
20. The trapeze artist appeared to be (fear)less.

Page 12

Answer Key

Page 13

Name _____

Capital Letters

The first word of every sentence must begin with a capital letter.

Use the words in the Word Bank to complete each sentence.

Word Bank

seven	trains	do	snow	presents
apples	blue	dogs	airplanes	clowns
		pair	coats	

Example ▷ <u>Twelve</u> inches make a foot.

1. <u>Dogs</u> are my favorite animals.
2. <u>Seven</u> days are in a week.
3. <u>Apples</u> are round and red.
4. <u>Trains</u> run on tracks.
5. <u>Airplanes</u> fly in the sky.
6. <u>Blue</u> is the color of the sky.
7. <u>Pair</u> means to have two.
8. <u>Do</u> you have any brothers?
9. <u>Clowns</u> make me laugh.
10. <u>Snow</u> falls in the winter.
11. <u>Coats</u> keep us warm.
12. <u>Presents</u> are fun to open.

Page 14

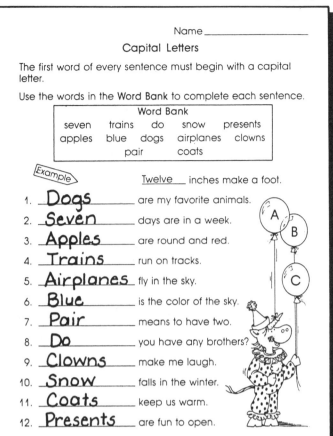

Name _____

Capital Letters

Use capital letters for names of people and pets. Use a capital letter to begin each word in a name.

Steven Alan Jones	Donald Duck
Lisa Marie Hayes	Minnie Mouse

Copy these names. Use capital letters where needed.

1. jane ellen smith <u>Jane Ellen Smith</u> (Example)
2. mickey mouse <u>Mickey Mouse</u>
3. paul mark cooper <u>Paul Mark Cooper</u>
4. mary sue ford <u>Mary Sue Ford</u>
5. snoopy <u>Snoopy</u>
6. david joseph moore <u>David Joseph Moore</u>
7. nancy lynn parker <u>Nancy Lynn Parker</u>
8. charlie brown <u>Charlie Brown</u>
9. kenny david gibson <u>Kenny David Gibson</u>
10. tom edward turner <u>Tom Edward Turner</u>
11. lassie <u>Lassie</u>
12. sara jane post <u>Sara Jane Post</u>
13. louisa mae williams <u>Louisa Mae Williams</u>
14. tabby <u>Tabby</u>

Page 15

Name _____

Capital Letters

Use a capital letter for a title in a name. Use a period after the abbreviation.

Mr. Sam Tucker   Dr. Helen Jean Bayer

Use a capital letter for an initial in a name. Use a period after the initial.

Tony L. Carter   Jill C. Dolan

Copy these sentences. Use capital letters and periods where needed.

1. mr jack m kent is my friend.

<u>Mr. Jack M. Kent is my friend.</u>

2. dr robert e lewis is my doctor.

<u>Dr. Robert E. Lewis is my doctor.</u>

3. mrs ann s sharp is my mother.

<u>Mrs. Ann S. Sharp is my mother.</u>

4. mindy gave me a minnie mouse coloring book.

<u>Mindy gave me a Minnie Mouse coloring book.</u>

5. george washington was our first president.

<u>George Washington was our first president.</u>

6. karen's dad is mr mark p simon.

<u>Karen's dad is Mr. Mark P. Simon.</u>

7. my teacher is mr vincent r williams.

<u>My teacher is Mr. Vincent R. Williams.</u>

Page 16

Name _____

Capital Letters

Capitalize...
- the first word of a sentence.   It is snowing.
- particular people and pets.   Sonia   Pluto
- titles and abbreviations.   Miss Holmes   Dr.
- particular places and things.   Symphony Hall   Freedom Trail
- the word I.   I am reading.

Copy the sentences below using capital letters where needed.

Example ▷ i'm going with mr. kent to tiger stadium.
<u>I'm going with Mr. Kent to Tiger Stadium.</u>

1. lisa and terry went to see dr. stan young.

<u>Lisa and Terry went to see Dr. Stan Young.</u>

2. i live on the corner of belt ave. and boise dr.

<u>I live on the corner of Belt Ave. and Boise Dr.</u>

3. my dog's name is pancake.

<u>My dog's name is Pancake.</u>

4. did you watch johnny carson last night?

<u>Did you watch Johnny Carson last night?</u>

5. mr. jackson works at the metropolitan museum.

<u>Mr. Jackson works at the Metropolitan Museum.</u>

6. i got presents for aunt emily and uncle jim.

<u>I got presents for Aunt Emily and Uncle Jim.</u>

7. cathy and i went to the lincoln memorial.

<u>Cathy and I went to the Lincoln Memorial.</u>

8. the st. louis cardinals will be in the play-offs.

<u>The St. Louis Cardinals will be in the play-offs.</u>

Answer Key

Page 17

Name _____

Capital Letters

Names of months, special days and holidays begin with capital letters.

January New Year's Day	February	March	April
1. *Martin Luther King Day*	*Valentine's Day* 2.	*St. Patrick's Day* 3.	*April Fool's Day* 4. *Easter*
May Memorial Day 5. *Mother's Day*	June *Flag Day* 6. *Father's Day*	July *Indepen-dence Day* 7.	August *Friendship Day* 8.
September Labor Day 9.	October *Columbus Day* *Halloween* 10. *United Nations Day*	November *Thanksgiving* *Veteran's Day* 11.	December *Christmas* *Hanukkah* 12.

> Example

Rewrite these months, special days and holidays. Put them on the calendar in order. Use capital letters where needed.

1. january—new year's day
   martin luther king day

2. february—valentine's day

3. march—st. patrick's day

4. april—april fool's day
   easter

5. may—memorial day
   mother's day

6. june—flag day
   father's day

7. july—independence day

8. august—friendship day

9. september—labor day

10. october—columbus day
    halloween
    united nations day

11. november—thanksgiving
    veteran's day

12. december—christmas
    hanukkah

Page 17

Page 18

Name _____

Capital Letters

Capitalize...
- cities, states, countries.   Tulsa, Oklahoma, United States
- lakes, rivers, oceans.   Blue River   Indian Ocean
- holidays.   Thanksgiving
- days of the week and months.   Monday   June
- names for people of particular countries.   French

Copy the sentences below using capital letters where needed.

> Example
> The third sunday in june is father's day.
> The third Sunday in June is Father's Day.

1. The mississippi river is east of st. louis, missouri.
   The Mississippi River is east of St. Louis, Missouri.

2. Many spanish people live in houston, texas.
   Many Spanish people live in Houston, Texas.

3. Valentine's day is celebrated february 14th.
   Valentine's Day is celebrated February 14th.

4. School starts the first tuesday after labor day.
   School starts the first Tuesday after Labor Day.

5. I swam in lake michigan when I was in chicago, illinois.
   I swam in Lake Michigan when I was in Chicago, Illinois.

6. I visited london, england last july.
   I visited London, England last July.

7. hoover dam and lake mead are near las vegas.
   Hoover Dam and Lake Mead are near Las Vegas.

8. Last monday, august 17, was my birthday.
   Last Monday, August 17, was my birthday.

Page 18

Page 19

Name _____

Capital Letters

Capitalize most words in a book title. Always capitalize the first word and the last word. Do not capitalize little words, such as: the, in, to, at.

The Fox and the Hound

Write one of the following book titles on each book.

the egg and i
railroads of the world
cinderella
cat in the hat
jack and the beanstalk

goldilocks and the three bears
the story of george washington
alice in wonderland
how to write reports
jokes and riddles

The Egg and I (Example) | Railroads of the World | Cinderella | Cat in the Hat | Jack and the Beanstalk

Goldilocks and the Three Bears | The Story of George Washington | How to Write Reports | Alice in Wonderland | Jokes and Riddles

Page 19

Page 20

Name _____

Capital Letters

Capitalize...
- titles of T.V. programs, movies, books and poems except for small words like: and, of, in, the. Always capitalize the first and last words.   Dungeons and Dragons
- Copy the title below the book, T.V. screen or movie screen using capital letters where needed.

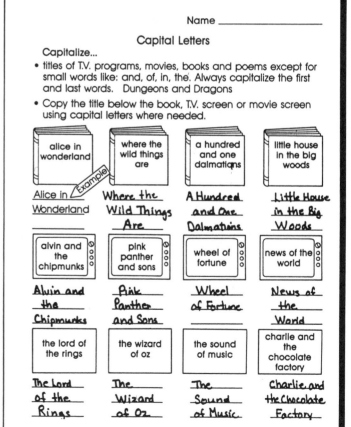

| alice in wonderland (Example) | where the wild things are | a hundred and one dalmatians | little house in the big woods |
| Alice in Wonderland | Where the Wild Things Are | A Hundred and One Dalmatians | Little House in the Big Woods |

| alvin and the chipmunks | pink panther and sons | wheel of fortune | news of the world |
| Alvin and the Chipmunks | Pink Panther and Sons | Wheel of Fortune | News of the World |

| the lord of the rings | the wizard of oz | the sound of music | charlie and the chocolate factory |
| The Lord of the Rings | The Wizard of Oz | The Sound of Music | Charlie and the Chocolate Factory |

Page 20

Answer Key

Page 21

Name _____

Capital Letters
Review
All About Me

Complete each sentence using capital letters where needed.
Don't forget the periods. **(answers will vary)**

1. My name is _____

2. The date I was born is _____

3. I live in the city of _____ in the state
   of _____ in the country of_____

4. My favorite book is _____

5. My favorite holiday is _____

6. My favorite pet's name is _____

7. My favorite movie is _____

8. My best friend is _____

9. My favorite teacher is _____

10. My favorite day of the week is _____ because
    _____

11. My favorite song is _____

12. The names of my family members are:

    _____ _____ _____

    _____ _____ _____

Page 22

Name _____

Capital Letters

Capitalize...

- the first word of a direct quotation.   "Can you play?" asked Jane.
- the first word in a greeting of a letter.   Dear Ned,
- The first word in the closing of a letter.   Your friend, Tracy

Copy the sentences below using capital letters where needed.

Example > My letter began, dear aunt carol.
My letter began, Dear Aunt Carol.

1. Dad said, "barry, let's play ball."
   Dad said, "Barry, let's play ball."

2. The teacher asked, "have you finished your homework?"
   The teacher asked, "Have you finished your homework?"

3. My note ended, your friend, nina.
   My note ended, Your friend, Nina.

4. "that's it," said Sean. "that's the right answer."
   "That's it," said Sean. "That's the right answer."

5. Mother's note to my teacher began, dear miss black.
   Mother's note to my teacher began, Dear Miss Black.

6. "I got a new bike!" yelled Erik.
   "I got a new bike!" yelled Erik.

7. The thank you note ended, gratefully, mrs. shea.
   The thank you note ended, Gratefully, Mrs. Shea.

8. I whispered, "be quiet, the baby is sleeping."
   I whispered, "Be quiet, the baby is sleeping."

Page 23

Name _____

Capital Letters Review

A B C D E F

In the sentences below, circle the words that should begin with a capital letter.

Example > (is) "(i) (love) (lucy)" still on television?

1. "(after) lunch," said (sue), "let's go shopping."
2. (i) learned a lot from the book, (inside) (the) (personal) (computer).
3. (my) class from (hudson) (school) went to (forest) (park).
4. (carlos) speaks (spanish), (french), and (english).
5. (the) (carter) family lives on (terrace) (drive).
6. "(the) (new) (kid) on the (block)" is a great story.
7. (we) saw the movie "(ghostbusters)" last (saturday).
8. (christopher) (columbus) (discovered) (america) in 1492.
9. (i) was born (june) 12, 1965, in (denver), (colorado).
10. (next) (thursday), (mr.) and (mrs.) (evans) have an anniversary.
11. (my) brother will attend (harvard) (college) in (boston).
12. (the) (letter) to (montie) ended, (love) from, (aunt) (rose).
13. (in) (hawaii), (kamehameka) (day) is celebrated each (june).
14. (mrs.) (hardy) said, "(don't) be late for the party."
15. (stone) (brothers) (hardware) is on (elm) (street).

Page 24

Sentences This is my bone.

Name _____

A sentence is a group of words that tells a complete idea.

The dictionaries are on the bottom shelf.

Not all groups of words are sentences. This group of words does not tell a complete idea.

The dictionaries on the bottom shelf

If the group of words below tells a complete idea, write S for sentence on the line. If it does not tell a complete idea, write NS for not a sentence. Add periods if the group of words is a sentence.

Example > ___S___ Carla ate her dinner.

Example > ___NS___ After the ballgame

1. __S__ The grass is green.
2. __NS__ The English test tomorrow
3. __NS__ After the ballgame
4. __NS__ The blue sweater in my drawer
5. __S__ It is snowing.
6. __S__ Matt and Jimmy are twins.
7. __NS__ Under the desk my cat
8. __S__ Derek visited Mexico.
9. __NS__ The puzzle on the table
10. __S__ Julie dressed her doll.

Answer Key

Page 25

Sentences   Name _____

Remember: A sentence contains a complete thought.

For each group of words below, write a complete sentence, putting the words in the correct order.

Answers will vary.

Example ▷ squirrel tree the gray our in little lives
The little gray squirrel lives in our tree.

1. a in tied Billy knot string the
   Billy tied a knot in the string.

2. brought party each something the child for
   Each child brought something for the party.

3. children street on the play kickball my
   The children play kickball on my street.

4. student new this is year Joanie a
   Joanie is a new student this year.

5. favorite red my roses are flowers bright
   My favorite flowers are bright, red roses.

6. new dentist gave toothbrush the me a
   The dentist gave me a new toothbrush.

7. was with steak mushrooms our served brown
   Our steak was served with brown mushrooms.

8. my took cleaners the I coat to
   I took my coat to the cleaners.

9. ticket name the it had lucky Susie's on
   The lucky ticket had Susie's name on it.

Page 25

Page 26

Sentences   Name _____

A sentence is a group of words that contains a complete thought.

Every sentence has two parts. The subject tells who or what did something. The predicate tells what the subject does or did, or what the subject is or has.

Rachel   has a new bike.
who   has

The Drama Club   meets every Wednesday.
what   does

In the sentences below, draw one line under the subject and two lines under the predicate.

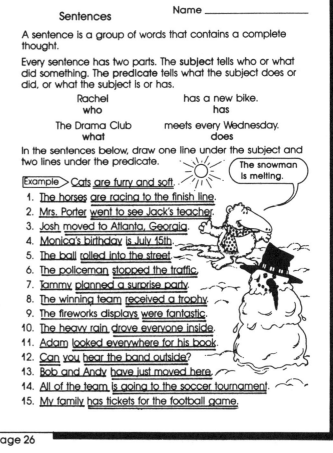

The snowman is melting.

Example ▷ Cats are furry and soft.

1. The horses are racing to the finish line.
2. Mrs. Porter went to see Jack's teacher.
3. Josh moved to Atlanta, Georgia.
4. Monica's birthday is July 15th.
5. The ball rolled into the street.
6. The policeman stopped the traffic.
7. Tammy planned a surprise party.
8. The winning team received a trophy.
9. The fireworks displays were fantastic.
10. The heavy rain drove everyone inside.
11. Adam looked everywhere for his book.
12. Can you hear the band outside?
13. Bob and Andy have just moved here.
14. All of the team is going to the soccer tournament.
15. My family has tickets for the football game.

Page 26

Page 27

Sentences
Subjects Predicates   Name _____

Every sentence has two parts which are called subject and predicate. The subject tells who or what does something. The predicate tells what the subject does, what the subject is or what the subject has.

The train   goes on tracks.
what   does

That song   is my favorite.
what   is

My friend   has new ice skates.
who   has

In the sentences below, draw one line under the subject and two lines under the predicate.

Example ▷ The cows are in the pasture.

1. The telephone was for me.
2. Mother baked a pumpkin pie.
3. Alison fed the baby animals.
4. The Indians passed the peace pipe.
5. The garden needs water to grow.
6. Lisa has beautiful long hair.
7. Doug and Ben played tennis.
8. Our family went apple picking.
9. The washing machine was broken.
10. My grandparents called me on my birthday.
11. Alex bought a new computer game.
12. We went on a float trip last summer.

Page 27

Page 28

Sentences
Subjects Predicates   Name _____
               Review

Write a complete sentence using each of the following subjects.

Example ▷ Miss Piggy likes purple gloves

1. The bears (answers will vary)
2. The tunnel _____
3. Stan _____
4. My camera _____
5. Snoopy _____
6. Dana and Andrea _____
7. Thanksgiving _____

Write a complete sentence using each of the following predicates.

Example ▷ The banana split was wonderful.

1. (Answers will vary) made me laugh.
2. _____ is ten miles away.
3. _____ plays the piano.
4. _____ grows very well.
5. _____ woke up the campers.
6. _____ was brand new.
7. _____ are bright red.

Page 28

Answer Key

Page 29

Sentences
Subject/Predicate   Review

Name _____

Write a complete sentence using each of the following subjects.

Example> The magician <u>performs difficult tricks</u>.

1. The truck _____
2. Mr. and Mrs. Turner _____
3. The clowns _____
4. Fresh strawberries _____
5. Our team _____
6. A large crowd _____
7. Pancakes _____
8. All of the joggers _____
9. The skeleton _____

Write a complete sentence using each of the following predicates.

Example> ___ The busy street ___ was noisy.
1. _____ was funny.
2. _____ will be ready.
3. _____ went too quickly.
4. _____ is on the corner.
5. _____ were ruined.
6. _____ still exists.
7. _____ was fun.
8. _____ were on my desk.
9. _____ turned to gold.

Page 29

Page 30

Sentences

A sentence must answer these two questions.

Who or what did something? What happened?

Robert forgot his lunch.

Not all groups of words are sentences.

Forgot his lunch

Decide if each of the following groups of words answers both questions; who or what did something and what happened. After each group of words write **S** for sentence or **NS** for not a sentence. Add a period if it is a sentence.

Example> The largest tigers in the world   **NS**
Example> We will visit Mexico.   **S**
1. The present was wrapped.   **S**
2. Andrea swam very fast.   **S**
3. A very funny comic book   **NS**
4. Found and buried the nut   **NS**
5. They ride horses.   **S**
6. A speedboat on the lake   **NS**
7. On Saturday, around the house   **NS**
8. That joke was not funny.   **S**
9. Lost her favorite ring at the store   **NS**
10. During the Middle Ages, Robin Hood   **NS**
11. Finally finished the job   **NS**
12. The rocket landed yesterday.   **S**
13. The tiny baby lying quietly in the cradle   **NS**

*On the back of your paper, rewrite the groups of words that were not sentences so they contain a complete thought.

Page 30

Page 31

Sentences
Statement or Question?

Name _____

Each kind of sentence does a different job. A statement is a sentence that tells something. It ends with a period.

I study French. [•]

A question is a sentence that asks something. It ends with a question mark.

Do you study French? [?]

Decide if each sentence below is a statement or a question. Write the answer on the line. Put the correct ending mark at the end of each sentence.

Example> Did you finish your homework?   <u>question</u>
Example> Our grass needs cutting.   <u>statement</u>

1. Our company is coming soon.   1. **statement**
2. Sarah wore a heavy sweater.   2. **statement**
3. Is that your lunchbox?   3. **question**
4. May I have some popcorn?   4. **question**
5. The music was too loud.   5. **statement**
6. When is your birthday?   6. **question**
7. Have you seen Erik?   7. **question**
8. I need a map to get home.   8. **statement**
9. Where is your notebook?   9. **question**
10. I need $1.00 for lunch.   10. **statement**

Page 31

Page 32

Questions
Statements

Name _____

In each picture are two children. Give them each a name. Write a question one child might be asking the other. Place a question mark after each question.

Write the answer of the second child. Place a period after your answer.

(answers will vary)

Names: _____ and _____
Question: _____
Answer: _____

Names: _____ and _____
Question: _____
Answer: _____

Names: _____ and _____
Question: _____
Answer: _____

Names: _____ and _____
Question: _____
Answer: _____

On another sheet of paper, write 5 questions for a friend to answer.

Page 32

Answer Key

Page 33

Name_____

Sentences
Exclamation or Command?

A command is a sentence that tells someone to do something. A command ends with a period.

Stop talking. •

An exclamation is a sentence that shows strong feelings, such as anger or excitement. It ends with an exclamation point.

This is so wonderful! !

Decide if each sentence below is a command or an exclamation. Write your answer on the line. Put the correct ending mark at the end of each sentence.

Example> Jill, feed the dog.   command

Example> I hate peas!   exclamation

1. Don't be late for your lesson.   1. **command**
2. Answer the door.   2. **command**
3. This water is too hot!   3. **exclamation**
4. Tony, make your bed.   4. **command**
5. It's freezing in here!   5. **exclamation**
6. Get up at 7:00 a.m. tomorrow.   6. **command**
7. Your grades are marvelous!   7. **exclamation**
8. Hang up your clothes.   8. **command**
9. This surprise party is great!   9. **exclamation**
10. Those elephants are enormous!   10. **exclamation**

Page 33

Page 34

Can you play?   Hurry up!   Name_____   I ate an apple.

Question Marks
Periods
Exclamation Points

A period is used...
- at the end of statements and commands.
- after an initial in a name.
- after many abbreviations.

We went home.
F.D. Roosevelt
Dr. Ave. In. Co.

A question mark is used...
- at the end of a question.   Did you mail my letter?

An exclamation point is used...
- after an exclamation or command that shows strong feelings.   Come quickly!

In the following sentences, use periods, question marks and exclamation points where they are needed.

Example> Lt. Stanley R. Mayberry is my uncle.

1. Thurs. Sept. 7. is my birthday.
2. My neighbor works at J. C. Penney Co.
3. Can you run a mi. in 15 minutes ?
4. Will you take a train to St. Louis ?
5. Eat your dinner !
6. The room measured 25 ft. 4 in. in length.
7. Did Carla move to Price Dr. last July ?
8. Main St. and 5th Ave. is where Sara lives.
9. Hurry up and finish that right now !
10. Rev. and Mrs R. W. Gordon live next door.
11. I bought a doz. apples for Ms. Haley.
12. My appointment with Dr. Rosen is at 2:30 P.M.
13. The baby was born at 6 A.M. and weighed 9 lbs. 13 oz.

Page 34

Page 35

Name_____

Common Nouns

A noun is a word that names a:

person   or   place   or   thing

Fill in each blank with a noun.

1. My **dog** was barking.
2. I like **apples** to eat.
3. **Ice** is extremely cold.
4. A **rainbow** has many colors.
5. The red **flower** is pretty.
6. The living room **lamp** is on.
7. John rode the **bus** to school.
8. Sally read her favorite **book**.
9. She had a **smile** on her face.
10. I sat in a comfortable **chair**.
11. I play the **flute** well.
12. The **policeman** captured the robber.
13. Bob played outside in the **park**

Page 35

Page 36

Name_____

Proper Nouns

A noun that names a particular person, place or thing is a proper noun. Proper nouns begin with capital letters.

Dr. John Smith   Mulberry Street   Mount Everest

Read the following sentences. Write the proper nouns from each sentence on the scoreboard below. Be sure to begin each proper noun with a capital letter.

1. My friend, carol, is from houston, texas.
2. I sent a letter to uncle charlie.
3. I watched mister ed on television.
4. The lincoln memorial is in washington d c.
5. My aunt mary took me to see "star wars".
6. In 1492, columbus discovered america.
7. Our first president was george washington.
8. I live on fifth street in new york.
9. I saw dr. tom holmes when I was sick.
10. We camped in yellowstone national park.

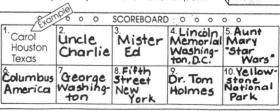

Mulberry Street

SCOREBOARD

1. *Example* Carol Houston Texas	2. Uncle Charlie	3. Mister Ed	4. Lincoln Memorial Washington, D.C.	5. Aunt Mary "Star Wars"
6. Columbus America	7. George Washington	8. Fifth Street New York	9. Dr. Tom Holmes	10. Yellowstone National Park

Page 36

Answer Key

Page 37

Common Nouns / Proper Nouns

A common noun names a person, place or thing.
A common noun begins with a small letter.

dog   book

A proper noun names a particular person, place or thing.
A proper noun begins with a capital letter.

Lassie   Sleeping Beauty

Copy each of the following nouns into a bubble from the common noun pipe or proper noun pipe.

1. dentist
2. bear
3. snoopy
4. doctor
5. ohio
6. school
7. abe lincoln
8. pacific ocean
9. chief
10. peter pan
11. halloween
12. hotel
13. monday
14. piano

Page 38

Common Nouns / Proper Nouns — Review

Look at the list of nouns. If it is a common noun, copy it in the cloud titled common nouns. If it is a proper noun, change its first letters to capital letters and copy it in the cloud titled proper nouns.

1. ohio
2. dr simon
3. ocean
4. president lincoln
5. dog
6. jane
7. new york
8. ice cream
9. mount everest
10. columbus
11. teacher
12. second avenue
13. circus
14. sheriff

Page 39

Plural Nouns

A singular noun names one person, place or thing.

APPLE

A plural noun names more than one person, place or thing. Usually, plural nouns have an S ending.

APPLES

When a singular noun ends in S-SH-CH- or X, add es to make the plural form.

S— losses	buses
SH— brushes	bushes
CH— peaches	bunches
X— boxes	foxes

Write the plural of each of the following.

car	pencil	dress	dish	bird
cars	pencils	dresses	dishes	birds
sandwich	six	balloon	ax	ball
sandwiches	sixes	balloons	axes	balls

Page 40

Plural Nouns

To form the plural of most nouns, add s.

bananas   chairs

When the singular form ends with s-sh-ch-x, add es.

boxes   peaches

Write the plural for each of the nouns on the chalkboard.

bunch	class	wax	fox
chair	brush	watch	pronoun
bus	fix	light	bus
plant	radio	push	wish
clock	pass	tax	switch
dish	church	report	press
witch	trick	patch	ticket

bunches (Example)	classes	waxes	foxes
chairs	brushes	watches	pronouns
buses	fixes	lights	buses
plants	radios	pushes	wishes
clocks	passes	taxes	switches
dishes	churches	reports	presses
witches	tricks	patches	tickets

Answer Key

Name _____

Plural Nouns

When a singular noun ends in a consonant and y, change the y to i and add es.

penny–pennies   fly–flies

Some singular nouns form their plural in special ways. There is no rule for these, so you have to memorize them.

man–men   woman–women   child–children
foot–feet   tooth–teeth   mouse–mice

Below is a chalkboard. Write the plural of each of the following words on the chalkboard.

1. bunny	5. mouse	9. man
2. pony	6. tooth	10. boy
3. foot	7. child	11. cherry
4. party	8. candy	12. woman

1. bunnies ‹Example
2. ponies
3. feet
4. parties
5. mice
6. teeth
7. children
8. candies
9. men
10. boys
11. cherries
12. women

Page 41

Name _____

Plural Nouns

When a singular noun ends in a consonant and y, change the y to i and add es.

daisy
daisies   butterfly
butterflies

To some nouns ending in f, simply add s.
chief–chiefs   bluff–bluffs

To other nouns ending in f or fe, change the f or fe to v and add es. You must memorize these as there is no rule.

calf–calves   knife–knives   loaf–loaves   life–lives
wolf–wolves   shelf–shelves   half–halves   leaf–leaves

Write the plural for each of the nouns below on the chalkboard.

1. dwarf	7. calf	13. sky
2. cherry	8. cuff	14. leaf
3. knife	9. lady	15. army
4. roof	10. wolf	16. fairy
5. life	11. half	17. shelf
6. baby	12. belief	18. loaf

1. dwarfs ‹Example
2. cherries
3. knives
4. roofs
5. lives
6. babies
7. calves
8. cuffs
9. ladies
10. wolves
11. halves
12. beliefs
13. skies
14. leaves
15. armies
16. fairies
17. shelves
18. loaves

Page 42

Name _____

Plural Nouns

These nouns are the same for both singular and plural. You will have to memorize them.

deer	salmon	trout	sheep	moose
tuna	cod	pike	bass	elk

These nouns form their plurals in special ways. You will have to memorize them.

goose–geese   man–men   woman–women   tooth–teeth
ox–oxen   foot–feet   child–children mouse–mice

Write the plural for each of the nouns below on the blanks.

1. cod	7. trout	13. tuna
2. goose	8. elk	14. man
3. salmon	9. ox	15. child
4. woman	10. deer	16. bass
5. moose	11. foot	17. mouse
6. tooth	12. pike	18. sheep

1. cod ‹Example
2. geese
3. salmon
4. women
5. moose
6. teeth
7. trout
8. elk
9. oxen
10. deer
11. feet
12. pike
13. tuna
14. men
15. children
16. bass
17. mice
18. sheep

Page 43

Name _____

Plural Nouns
Review

Follow the path around. Write the plural for each noun.

Start

fish — fish
box — boxes
party — parties
house — houses
clock — clocks
baby — babies
lunch — lunches
class — classes
pass — passes
mouse — mice
man — men
foot — feet
pony — ponies
broom — brooms
board — boards
wish — wishes

End

Page 44

Page 45

Name _____

Plural Nouns Review

Write the plural for each of the nouns below.

wish *Example*	hobby	sheep	day
wishes	_hobbies_	_sheep_	_days_
deer	bluff	child	boss
deer	_bluffs_	_children_	_bosses_
rash	cookie	match	knife
rashes	_cookies_	_matches_	_knives_
car	success	pony	foot
cars	_successes_	_ponies_	_feet_
kiss	city	couch	mouse
kisses	_cities_	_couches_	_mice_
woman	half	mirror	trout
women	_halves_	_mirrors_	_trout_
person	tooth	dress	girl
persons	_teeth_	_dresses_	_girls_

Page 45

Page 46

Name _____

Possessive Nouns

A possessive noun shows ownership or possession. To make a singular noun show possession, add an **apostrophe** and s.

child's toy   teacher's book

Fill in the blank with a possessive noun.

Example the _dog's_ bone

1. the **bird's** nest
2. the **lion's** cage
3. the **flower's** petal
4. the **snow-man's** nose

To make a plural noun that ends in s show possession, add an apostrophe after the s.

dogs' bones

To make a plural noun that does not end in s show possession, add an apostrophe and s.

children's games

Fill in each blank with a possessive noun.

Example the _dogs'_ tails

1. the **chairs'** legs
2. the **fire-men's** hoses
3. the **cats'** tails
4. the **books'** pages

Page 46

Page 47

Name _____

Possessive Nouns

A possessive noun is a noun that shows ownership.

To make a singular noun show possession, add an apostrophe and s.

farmer's rake   garden's flower

If a plural noun ends in s, simply add an apostrophe.

farmers' rakes   gardens' flowers

If a plural noun does not end in s, add an apostrophe and s.

men's shoes   women's shoes

Write each group of words to make them show ownership.

Example the report card of Paul   Paul's report card

1. the toys of the children — _the children's toys_
2. the tail of the monkey — _the monkey's tail_
3. the cages of the animals — _the animals' cages_
4. the balls of the bowlers — _the bowlers' balls_
5. the house of my friend — _my friend's house_
6. the uniforms of the players — _the players' uniforms_
7. the backpack of Joan — _Joan's backpack_
8. the shoes of the runners — _the runners' shoes_
9. the paintings of the artist — _the artist's paintings_
10. the monitor of the computer — _the computer's monitor_
11. the hats of the men — _the men's hats_
12. the wife of my boss — _my boss's wife_

Page 47

Page 48

Name _____

Possessive Nouns

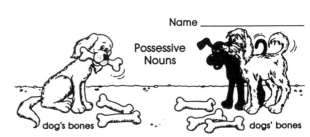

dog's bones   dogs' bones

Change the underlined word to show possession by adding an apostrophe or apostrophe and s. Write the possessive form on the line.

Possessive

Example <u>Sally</u> dress is blue — _Sally's_

1. Mother took me to <u>Tony</u> house. — _Tony's_
2. The <u>chickens</u> eggs were large. — _chickens'_
3. <u>Jonathan</u> bicycle needs new brakes. — _Jonathan's_
4. Follow the <u>team</u> rules. — _team's_
5. The <u>shoes</u> soles need repair. — _shoes'_
6. Mrs. <u>Thomas</u> car was in the driveway. — _Thomas'_
7. My <u>brother</u> story won first prize. — _brother's_
8. Our <u>neighbors</u> lawns need cutting. — _neighbors'_
9. <u>Ellen</u> paintings were on display. — _Ellen's_
10. The truck <u>drivers</u> routes were long. — _drivers'_
11. The <u>babies</u> toys are put away. — _babies'_
12. The <u>principal</u> office is small. — _principal's_
13. The <u>bird</u> nest is completed. — _bird's_
14. The <u>doctors</u> hours were long. — _doctors'_
15. The <u>painter</u> brushes were clean. — _painter's_

Page 48

Answer Key

Page 49

Name _____

Possessive Nouns
Review

Change the underlined word to show possession by adding an apostrophe or apostrophe and s. Write the possessive form on the line.

possessive

Example ▷ The <u>balloon</u> string is long.   balloon's

1. The three <u>cats</u> paws were wet.   1. **cats'**
2. <u>Mary</u> pencil was broken.   2. **Mary's**
3. Both <u>boys</u> grades were good.   3. **boys'**
4. This house is <u>Cliff</u> house.   4. **Cliff's**
5. <u>Tony</u> aunt came to visit.   5. **Tony's**
6. Some <u>flowers</u> leaves were large.   6. **flowers'**
7. We saw two <u>bears</u> tracks.   7. **bears'**
8. The <u>children</u> room was messy.   8. **children's**
9. My <u>sister</u> birthday is today.   9. **sister's**
10. The <u>clowns</u> acts made us laugh.   10. **clowns'**
11. Charlie Brown filled <u>Snoopy</u> dish.   11. **Snoopy's**
12. Mark joined the game with the <u>boys</u>.   12. **boys**
13. The baseball <u>players</u> uniforms are clean.   13. **players'**
14. The <u>dog</u> dish was empty.   14. **dog's**

Page 49

Page 50

Name _____

Verbs

Verbs are words that show action or say that something is.

> We sailed on Lake Michigan.
> I am ten years old.

In the sentences below, circle the verbs.

Example ▷ We (went) to a movie.
1. Dad (washed) his new car in the driveway.
2. Nancy (took) pictures with her new camera.
3. We (numbered) our paper from 1 to 10.
4. My friends (need) help with their homework.
5. Mother (answered) the doorbell in her apron.
6. I (lost) my new sweater at the game.
7. The students (did) their math on the board.
8. We (painted) our house white and green.
9. Steve (ran) the 100-yard dash in the race.
10. The whole class (laughed) at my jokes.
11. The chef (baked) delicious pies and cakes.
12. Judy (slipped) on the ice and broke her arm.
13. Keith (thought) about his upcoming vacation.
14. (Read) the second chapter by tomorrow.
15. We (looked) through the microscope.
16. The boys (ran) and (jumped) over the fence.
17. The squirrels (looked) at us and then (ran) away.
18. Math (is) the subject most difficult for me.
19. My twin sisters (are) in the seventh grade.
20. My family (was) in Colorado when our car (quit!)

$$\begin{array}{r} 4 \\ \times 3 \\ \hline 12 \end{array}$$

$$12-6=6$$

$$\begin{array}{r} 172 \\ + 18 \\ \hline 190 \end{array}$$

Page 50

Page 51

Name _____

Action Verbs

Action verbs tell what a person or thing does.

Birds fly.   Dogs run.

Some action verbs tell about actions you can see. Others tell about actions you cannot see.

I enjoyed the game.   We liked the show.

Circle the action verbs. Write them on the lines below.

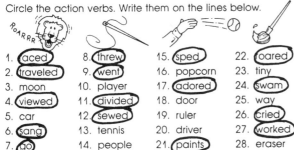

1. (raced)   8. (threw)   15. (sped)   22. (roared)
2. (traveled)   9. (went)   16. popcorn   23. tiny
3. moon   10. player   17. (adored)   24. (swam)
4. (viewed)   11. (divided)   18. door   25. way
5. car   12. (sewed)   19. ruler   26. (cried)
6. (sang)   13. tennis   20. driver   27. (worked)
7. (go)   14. people   21. (paints)   28. eraser

raced	go	sewed	roared
traveled	threw	sped	swam
viewed	went	adored	cried
sang	divided	paints	worked

Page 51

Page 52

Name _____

Helping Verbs

A helping verb is used with an action verb. The most important verb is called the main verb and usually comes last. All the other words in the verb are called helping verbs.

helping verbs	main verb
was	turning
should have	turned
must have been	turning

Study this wheel of helping verbs.

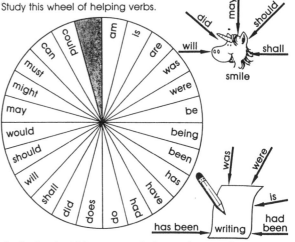

On the back of this paper, write ten sentences using helping verbs. Do not use a helping verb more than once.

Page 52

Grammar IF8730   115   © 1990 Instructional Fair, Inc.

Answer Key

Name _____

Helping Verbs

A verb may be a single word or a group of words. A verb with more than one word is made of a **main verb** and one or more **helping verbs**.

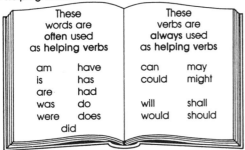

These words are often used as helping verbs		These verbs are always used as helping verbs	
am	have	can	may
is	has	could	
are	had		
was	do	will	shall
were	does	would	should
did			

In the following sentences, underline the main verb once and the helping verbs twice.

Today, I may read in class.

Example > I may have won first prize.

1. Maria might spend the night.
2. The flowers are growing tall.
3. Matt is playing the piano for the play.
4. They were going to the movie.
5. Freddie should listen in class.
6. Lori should have eaten her vegetables.
7. I will be twelve on my next birthday.
8. I can do my homework later.
9. Vince has been working much too hard.
10. When are you going to finish the book?

Page 53

Name _____

Helping Verbs

Usually verbs that end in **en** or **ing** need helping verbs.

I have written. I am writing.

In the following sentences, underline the main verb with one line. Underline the helping verbs with two lines.

Example > I have been swimming.

1. We were going to the tennis match.
2. The children have eaten lunch already.
3. They must have been sleeping soundly.
4. We could go to the circus on Saturday.
5. Uncle Harry has driven to Houston.
6. You are playing the piano very well.
7. Barry was studying for the test.
8. Chocolate sauce will be added to the dessert.
9. Jan has gone to the concert.
10. I am planning a party for my mother.
11. They have decided on a name for the baby.
12. Wendy may be riding her bike to school.
13. Carl and Gary should be coming soon.
14. I have been cutting the grass.

Page 54

Name _____

Helping Verbs

Always use helping verbs with **been, seen, done, gone**.

They **have been** ice skating.

Sometimes helping verbs and main verbs are separated by words that are not verbs.

Mike **can** usually **win** in Scrabble.

I have done well on my test.

In the following sentences, underline the main verb once and the helping verbs twice.

Example > My brother cannot drive yet.

1. Have you seen my new car?
2. Carlos did not tell anyone his secret.
3. I am usually working on Saturday.
4. Debbie has gone to the meeting at school.
5. She is not going swimming in the lake.
6. You should never chew gum in class.
7. Frank cannot get his locker open.
8. Did your older sister marry Tom?
9. I have been to my violin lesson.
10. I might not finish the large pizza.
11. Does the basketball game start at noon?
12. Tim can only play for one hour.
13. Was your mother angry about the window?
14. I am usually able to babysit on weekends.
15. I have never been to Hawaii, but I want to go!
16. Teaching school has always been my ambition.
17. Sara can often finish her homework before dinner.
18. Writing books is an enormous amount of work.

Have you read this book?

Page 55

Name _____

Verbs
Review

Underline the **whole verb** in each sentence below.

Example > We should be cooking dinner now.

1. The music was loud in the room.
2. Leon has been watering the grass.
3. Pedro has gone to school for four years.
4. We stood for the National Anthem.
5. Jill has eaten all the popcorn.
6. Katie and Julie are twins.
7. They have collected money for needy children.
8. Mary Lou will keep her cat inside.
9. Read the directions on the cover.

Circle the correct verb in each sentence below.

Example > Martin (am, (is)) my neighbor.

1. You ((were) was) excellent in the talent show.
2. Maria and Joanie ((are) was) going to the zoo.
3. The policeman ((is) are) directing traffic.
4. I ((was) is) eating pizza.
5. Craig (be, (has been)) packing for his trip.
6. I (is, (am)) doing a puzzle for my project.
7. The birds (was, (were)) singing outside my window.
8. The children ((are) is) dressing up for Halloween.

Page 56

Answer Key

Present Tense Verbs

Name_____

Review

Write the correct spelling for each verb in the clouds so it will show present tense. Use the s form.

- bury (Example) — buries
- wax — waxes
- wash — washes
- bite — bites
- speak — speaks
- like — likes
- catch — catches
- measure — measures
- boss — bosses

In the sentences below, circle the correct form of the verb.

Example > Jackie (carry, (carries)) her purse to school.

1. My father (shave, (shaves)) every day.
2. The chorus (sing, (sings)) beautifully.
3. The ice cream cones ((taste), tastes) delicious.
4. My neighbor (teach, (teaches)) French.
5. Meg (dash, (dashes)) to school every day.
6. The birds ((fly), flies) from tree to tree.
7. Elm Street (cross, (crosses)) Main Street.
8. Michael and Keith ((play), plays) tennis.
9. They ((wait), waits) for the bus at the corner.
10. The clowns ((make), makes) us laugh.

Page 57

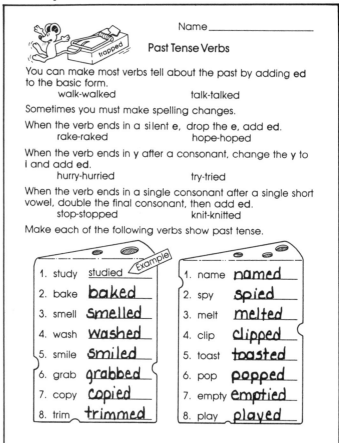

Past Tense Verbs

Name_____

You can make most verbs tell about the past by adding ed to the basic form.

walk-walked   talk-talked

Sometimes you must make spelling changes.

When the verb ends in a silent e, drop the e, add ed.

rake-raked   hope-hoped

When the verb ends in y after a consonant, change the y to i and add ed.

hurry-hurried   try-tried

When the verb ends in a single consonant after a single short vowel, double the final consonant, then add ed.

stop-stopped   knit-knitted

Make each of the following verbs show past tense.

1. study — studied (Example)
2. bake — baked
3. smell — smelled
4. wash — washed
5. smile — smiled
6. grab — grabbed
7. copy — copied
8. trim — trimmed

1. name — named
2. spy — spied
3. melt — melted
4. clip — clipped
5. toast — toasted
6. pop — popped
7. empty — emptied
8. play — played

Page 58

Past Tense Verbs

Name_____

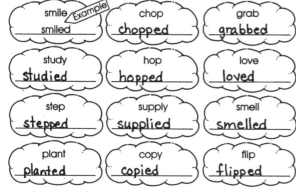
(begged) (dipped) (liked) (typed)

To make most verbs tell about the past, add ed to the basic form.

cook–cooked   clean–cleaned

When the verb ends in a silent e, drop the e and add ed.

rake–raked   hope–hoped

When the verb ends in y after a consonant, change the y to i and add ed.

bury–buried   spy–spied

When the verb ends in a single consonant after a single short vowel, double the final consonant and add ed.

clip–clipped   pop–popped

Write each of the following verbs using the correct ed ending.

- smile (Example) — smiled
- chop — chopped
- grab — grabbed
- study — studied
- hop — hopped
- love — loved
- step — stepped
- supply — supplied
- smell — smelled
- plant — planted
- copy — copied
- flip — flipped

Page 59

Past Tense With Helping Verbs

Name_____

Helping verbs can be used to tell about the past. Use **has** with a singular subject.

She has kicked the ball.

Use **have** with a plural subject or with I or you.

The boys have kicked the ball.

Use **had** with a singular or plural subject.

I had kicked the ball.   They had kicked the ball.

Write sentences with the following verbs using a helping verb and the correct ed ending. Use only **has** or **have**.

stare	We have stared all day long. (Example)
bake	_____
worry	_____
jump	_____
arrive	_____
fix	_____
reply	_____
step	_____
change	_____
try	_____
brag	_____
close	_____
open	_____
ski	_____

Page 60

Answer Key

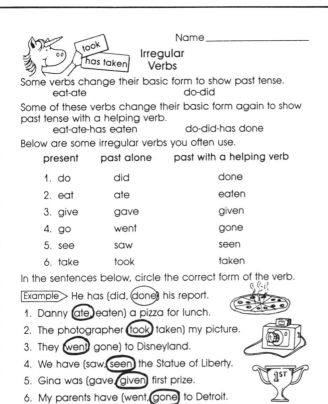

Page 61

Name _____

Irregular Verbs

Some verbs change their basic form to show past tense.

eat-ate   do-did

Some of these verbs change their basic form again to show past tense with a helping verb.

eat-ate-has eaten   do-did-has done

Below are some irregular verbs you often use.

present	past alone	past with a helping verb
1. do	did	done
2. eat	ate	eaten
3. give	gave	given
4. go	went	gone
5. see	saw	seen
6. take	took	taken

In the sentences below, circle the correct form of the verb.

Example> He has (did, **done**) his report.

1. Danny (**ate**, eaten) a pizza for lunch.
2. The photographer (**took**, taken) my picture.
3. They (**went**, gone) to Disneyland.
4. We have (saw, **seen**) the Statue of Liberty.
5. Gina was (gave, **given**) first prize.
6. My parents have (went, **gone**) to Detroit.
7. We (**saw**, seen) the greatest football game.
8. The class (**took**, taken) a field trip.

Page 62

Name _____

Irregular Verbs

Verbs that show past time in different ways are called irregular verbs.

Below are seven irregular verbs frequently used.

Present	Past-alone	Past with helping verb
break	broke	broken
bring	brought	brought
come	came	come
drive	drove	driven
do	did	done
eat	ate	eaten
give	gave	given

In the sentences below, circle the correct form of the verb.

Example> I have (did, **done**) the dishes.

1. We (**ate**, eaten) all the birthday cake.
2. Julie (**came**, come) to my piano recital.
3. Dad has (gave, **given**) me my allowance.
4. Mom (**drove**, driven) me to my soccer game.
5. Last night I (**did**, done) my homework.
6. My sister has (came, **come**) home from college.
7. My TV has been (broke, **broken**) a week.
8. Jimmy has (drove, **driven**) to Los Angeles.
9. Craig had (ate, **eaten**) too much ice cream.
10. I (**broke**, broken) my arm skiing in Colorado.
11. Elizabeth (**did**, done) me a big favor.
12. We have (gave, **given**) the problem much thought.
13. The Jordans (**gave**, give) a donation to the Red Cross.

Page 63

Name _____

Irregular Verbs

Below are seven more irregular verbs frequently used.

Present	Past-alone	Past with helping verb
grow	grew	grown
go	went	gone
run	ran	run
see	saw	seen
take	took	taken
throw	threw	thrown
write	wrote	written

In the sentences below, circle the correct form of the verb.

Example> Gavin has (grew, **grown**) two inches.

1. Our gym class (**ran**, run) the 50-yard dash.
2. My car should have (went, **gone**) to the repair shop.
3. Angela (**saw**, seen) the magic show.
4. Colin (**threw**, thrown) a snowball at Michael.
5. We have (ran, **run**) out of sugar.
6. Sharon has (wrote, **written**) a letter to Kathy.
7. We (**took**, taken) four rolls of film in Mexico.
8. We have (saw, **seen**) the Super Bowl.
9. After it rained, my flowers (**grew**, grown).
10. We (**went**, gone) on a cruise last July.
11. Have you (took, **taken**) out the trash?
12. I was (threw, **thrown**) off my horse.
13. Has the sick child (threw, **thrown**) up yet?
14. We had (went, **gone**) to Italy when it happened.

Page 64

Name _____

Past Tense Verbs
Review

Write the correct spelling for each verb in the clouds so it will show past tense.

taste (Example)	fry	fix
tasted	fried	fixed
knot	end	vote
knotted	ended	voted
raise	stop	rub
raised	stopped	rubbed

In the sentences below, circle the correct form of the verb.

Example> I (**did**, done) my homework.

1. You have (ate, **eaten**) too many cookies.
2. Donna had (saw, **seen**) the ice show.
3. We (**took**, taken) flowers to grandma.
4. Our family (**went**, gone) to the beach.
5. Josh should have (did, **done**) the dishes.
6. Have you been (gave, **given**) the assignment?
7. We (**ate**, eaten) popcorn at the movie.
8. Mother had (took, **taken**) Jeff to the dentist.
9. After it rained, we (**saw**, seen) a rainbow.
10. Dad had (went, **gone**) on a business trip.

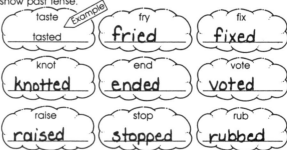

Answer Key

Page 65

Pronouns

Name_____

Pronouns are words that stand for singular or plural nouns.

Helpful Hints	singular	plural
pronouns used to talk about yourself	I, me	we, us
pronouns used to talk about the person	you	you
pronouns used to talk about other persons or things	he, him, it, she, her	they, them

Copy the pronoun from each sentence into the party favor next to the sentence.

Example> He is my only brother. — He

1. Nancy had her teeth cleaned. — her
2. Is mother going with us? — us
3. Do you like chocolate pie? — you
4. Tommy is taking him a present. — him
5. They watched the football game. — They
6. Dad gave them some money. — them
7. I watched cartoons on TV. — I
8. We went fishing yesterday. — we
9. Kathy gave me a present. — me
10. He bought a new game. — He

Page 65

Page 66

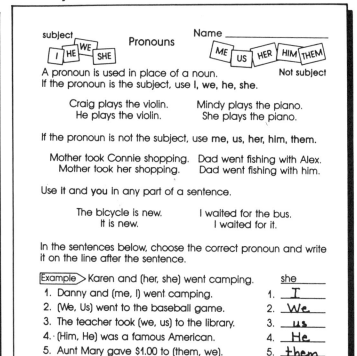

Pronouns

Name_____

A pronoun is used in place of a noun.
If the pronoun is the subject, use I, we, he, she.

Craig plays the violin.   Mindy plays the piano.
He plays the violin.   She plays the piano.

If the pronoun is not the subject, use me, us, her, him, them.

Mother took Connie shopping.   Dad went fishing with Alex.
Mother took her shopping.   Dad went fishing with him.

Use it and you in any part of a sentence.

The bicycle is new.   I waited for the bus.
It is new.   I waited for it.

In the sentences below, choose the correct pronoun and write it on the line after the sentence.

Example> Karen and (her, she) went camping. — she

1. Danny and (me, I) went camping. — 1. I
2. (We, Us) went to the baseball game. — 2. We
3. The teacher took (we, us) to the library. — 3. us
4. (Him, He) was a famous American. — 4. He
5. Aunt Mary gave $1.00 to (them, we). — 5. them
6. (Her, You) and Greg are my best friends. — 6. You
7. Please take this note to (he, him). — 7. him
8. Charlie took Alan and (me, I) to the party. — 8. me
9. The teacher told (she, her) to talk louder. — 9. her
10. You and (he, him) gave a good report. — 10. he

Page 66

Page 67

Name_____

Pronouns Review

In the following sentences, underline the pronouns. Write the noun or nouns the pronouns stand for on the blackboard below.

Example> Mary wore a blue dress. She spotted her dress.
1. The children played baseball. They won 6 to 2.
2. John and Tim raked leaves. Mother thanked them.
3. The dog ran in the street. Sally ran after him.
4. The boys saw a movie. It was scary.
5. The girls picked apples. Mother baked pies with them.
6. Freddy, would you please clean your room?
7. Mindy bought some peaches and paid $1.25 for them.
8. "Read me a poem, please," said Robin.
9. Sunshine is good for plants. It helps them grow.
10. Our class went on a trip. We had a picnic lunch.

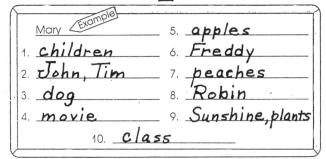

Mary (Example)
1. children
2. John, Tim
3. dog
4. movie
5. apples
6. Freddy
7. peaches
8. Robin
9. Sunshine, plants
10. class

Page 67

Page 68

Possessive Pronouns

Name_____

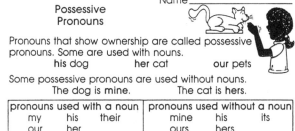

Pronouns that show ownership are called possessive pronouns. Some are used with nouns.
his dog   her cat   our pets
Some possessive pronouns are used without nouns.
The dog is mine.   The cat is hers.

pronouns used with a noun			pronouns used without a noun		
my	his	their	mine	his	its
our	her		ours	hers	
your	its		yours	theirs	

Write a new sentence using a possessive pronoun in place of the underlined words.

Example> Is this coat your coat?
Is this coat yours?

1. This house is Cliff's house.
   This house is his.
2. Nancy's friends came for dinner.
   Her friends came for dinner.
3. Angela and Jane's school is large.
   Their school is large.
4. That bicycle is my bicycle.
   That bicycle is mine.
5. This game is your game.
   This game is yours.
6. Pancake is Bill's dog.
   Pancake is his.

Page 68

Answer Key

Page 69

Name _____

Possessive Pronouns

The possessive form of a pronoun does not use an apostrophe. These are the possessive forms of pronouns.

my, mine	our, ours
your, yours	you, yours
his, her, hers, its	their, theirs

The dog lost its tag.   The twins rode their bikes.

In the following sentences, write the possessive pronoun on the line. Follow the information in the parentheses.

Example ▷ The bracelet is __mine__ .
(The bracelet belongs to me.)

1. Comb __your__ hair.
(The hair belongs to you.)

2. The baby took __its__ bottle.
(The bottle belongs to the baby.)

3. The books were __his__ .
(The books belonged to Jim.)

4. __Its__ fur was wet.
(The fur belonged to the dog.)

5. The mailman brought __our__ mail.
(The mail belonged to us.)

6. __My__ flowers are in bloom.
(The flowers belong to me.)

7. The blue bicycle is __yours__ .
(The bicycle belongs to you.)

8. __Her__ piano lesson is today.
(The piano lesson is Jill's.)

9. __Our__ TV set is broken.
(The TV belongs to us.)

That banana is yours.

This banana is mine.

Page 70

Name _____

Pronouns Review

Circle the pronouns in the following story. There are 24 pronouns.

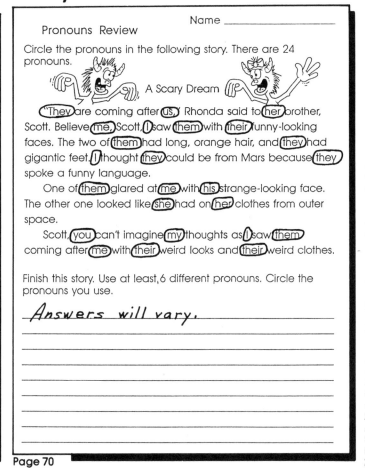

A Scary Dream

"(They) are coming after (us)," Rhonda said to (her) brother, Scott. Believe (me), Scott, (I) saw (them) with (their) funny-looking faces. The two of (them) had long, orange hair, and (they) had gigantic feet. (I) thought (they) could be from Mars because (they) spoke a funny language.

One of (them) glared at (me) with (his) strange-looking face. The other one looked like (she) had on (her) clothes from outer space.

Scott, (you) can't imagine (my) thoughts as (I) saw (them) coming after (me) with (their) weird looks and (their) weird clothes.

Finish this story. Use at least 6 different pronouns. Circle the pronouns you use.

Answers will vary.

Page 71

Name _____

Adjectives

An adjective is a word that describes a noun.

Adjectives ⟩ tell what kind
tell how many
tell which ones

bright sun
two birds
this tree

Complete each sentence below with an adjective that would describe each picture.

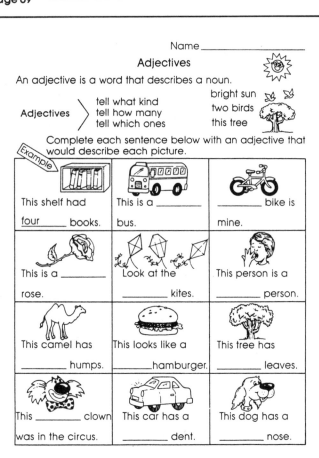

Example ▷

This shelf had __four__ books.	This is a _____ bus.	_____ bike is mine.
This is a _____ rose.	Look at the _____ kites.	This person is a _____ person.
This camel has _____ humps.	This looks like a _____ hamburger.	This tree has _____ leaves.
This _____ clown was in the circus.	This car has a _____ dent.	This dog has a _____ nose.

Page 72

Name _____

this
one
shiny
silver
that

key

four
gold
pretty
small
these

Adjectives

fishes

An adjective is a word that describes a noun or pronoun.

Adjectives...
• tell **what kind.**   kitchen table   card table
• tell **how many.**   seven pencils   many pencils
• tell **which ones.**   this   that   these   those

In the following sentences, write an adjective on each line. Do not use an adjective more than one time. Answers will vary.

Example ▷ My __older__ brother has a __blue__ bicycle.

1. My _____ skirt is plaid.   **Answers will vary.**
2. My _____ friend has _____ eyes.
3. The _____ weather was good for our garden.
4. _____ hat keeps my head warm.
5. The campers put up _____ tents.
6. Ben went to a _____ movie.
7. Mother picked up our _____ toys and _____ clothes.
8. We made a _____ , _____ vase in art class.
9. Dad is a _____ tennis player.
10. We saw _____ bears and _____ monkeys at the zoo.
11. Holly used her _____ calculator.
12. Our _____ dog is a _____ pet.
13. That _____ building is very _____ .
14. Sarah just got a _____ car and a _____ dog.
15. The _____ , _____ music drove my mom crazy.

Answer Key

Page 73

Adjectives

Name _____

Write five adjectives that could describe the picture in the center of each flower. Do not use an adjective more than one time.

Answers will vary.

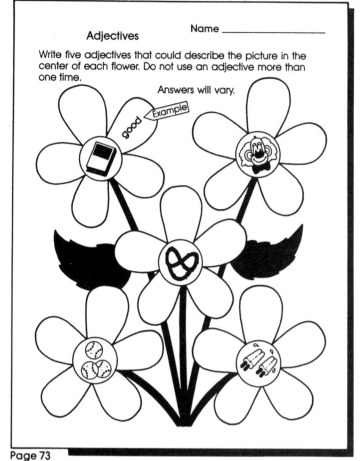

Page 74

Review

Name _____

Adjectives

Write three adjectives that describe each noun shown below. Do not use an adjective more than once.

book	feet	house
long ‹Example	_____	_____
good	_____	_____
true	_____	_____
airplane	hot dog	cloud
_____	_____	_____
_____	_____	_____
_____	_____	_____
butterflies	shoes	bells
_____	_____	_____
_____	_____	_____
_____	_____	_____
clown	flowers	ice cream cone
_____	_____	_____
_____	_____	_____
_____	_____	_____

Page 75

Name _____

fluffy cloud   **Adjectives**   rain cloud

Fill in the blanks with an adjective. Be creative.

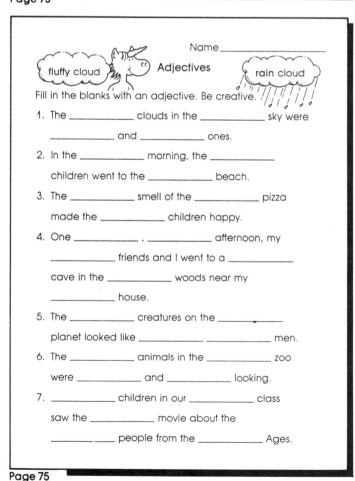

1. The _____ clouds in the _____ sky were _____ and _____ ones.

2. In the _____ morning, the _____ children went to the _____ beach.

3. The _____ smell of the _____ pizza made the _____ children happy.

4. One _____ , _____ afternoon, my _____ friends and I went to a _____ cave in the _____ woods near my _____ house.

5. The _____ creatures on the _____ planet looked like _____ _____ men.

6. The _____ animals in the _____ zoo were _____ and _____ looking.

7. _____ children in our _____ class saw the _____ movie about the _____ people from the _____ Ages.

Page 76

Name _____

Nouns   Adjectives
Review

Underline the adjective in each sentence. Circle the noun it describes. Write the adjective and the noun it describes on the lines after the sentence.

	adjective	noun
Example › Kevin's (bike) is blue.	blue	bike
1. Billy likes hot (cocoa.)	hot	cocoa
2. Mr. Atkins ran in two (marathons)	two	marathons
3. These (cookies) got burned.	burned	cookies
4. We peeled many (apples)	many	apples
5. Tina has brown (eyes)	brown	eyes
6. We looked around the ugly (room)	ugly	room
7. They ate fried (chicken.)	fried	chicken
8. Molly prefers pumpkin (pie.)	pumpkin	pie
9. I painted with water (colors)	water	colors
10. Ellen went to a surprise (party)	surprise	party
11. Patrick read mystery (books)	mystery	books
12. Take this (package) home.	this	package
13. We went in a new (airplane.)	new	airplane
14. Beth is very (pretty.)	very	pretty
15. We went to buy new (clothes)	new	clothes

Answer Key

Page 77

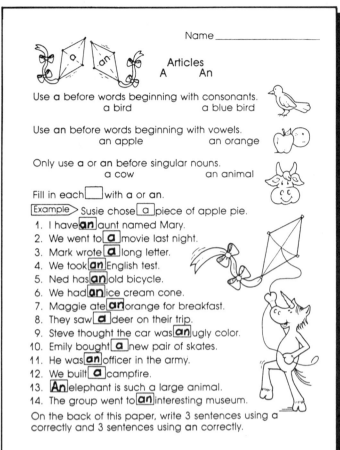

Articles
A   An

Name _____

Use **a** before words beginning with consonants.
a bird   a blue bird

Use **an** before words beginning with vowels.
an apple   an orange

Only use **a** or **an** before singular nouns.
a cow   an animal

Fill in each ☐ with a or an.

Example ➤ Susie chose **a** piece of apple pie.
1. I have **an** aunt named Mary.
2. We went to **a** movie last night.
3. Mark wrote **a** long letter.
4. We took **an** English test.
5. Ned has **an** old bicycle.
6. We had **an** ice cream cone.
7. Maggie ate **an** orange for breakfast.
8. They saw **a** deer on their trip.
9. Steve thought the car was **an** ugly color.
10. Emily bought **a** new pair of skates.
11. He was **an** officer in the army.
12. We built **a** campfire.
13. **An** elephant is such a large animal.
14. The group went to **an** interesting museum.

On the back of this paper, write 3 sentences using a correctly and 3 sentences using an correctly.

Page 77

Page 78

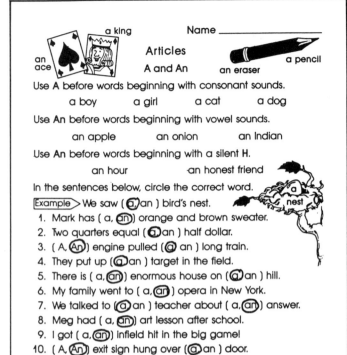

Articles
A and An

Name _____

a king
an ace
an eraser
a pencil

Use **A** before words beginning with consonant sounds.
a boy   a girl   a cat   a dog

Use **An** before words beginning with vowel sounds.
an apple   an onion   an Indian

Use **An** before words beginning with a silent H.
an hour   an honest friend

In the sentences below, circle the correct word.

Example ➤ We saw (**a**, an) bird's nest.
1. Mark has (a, **an**) orange and brown sweater.
2. Two quarters equal (**a**, an) half dollar.
3. (A, **An**) engine pulled (**a**, an) long train.
4. They put up (**a**, an) target in the field.
5. There is (a, **an**) enormous house on (**a**, an) hill.
6. My family went to (a, **an**) opera in New York.
7. We talked to (**a**, an) teacher about (a, **an**) answer.
8. Meg had (a, **an**) art lesson after school.
9. I got (a, **an**) infield hit in the big game!
10. (A, **An**) exit sign hung over (**a**, an) door.
11. We had (a, **an**) aunt and (a, **an**) uncle for dinner.
12. We had (**a**, an) cookie and (a, **an**) ice cream cone.
13. Vince ran for (a, **an**) hour on (**a**, an) cinder track.
14. Jim learned (a, **an**) Indian dance on (**a**, an) reservation.
15. (A, **An**) honest friend is someone to treasure.

Page 78

Page 79

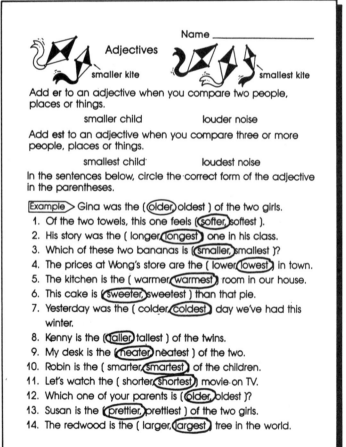

Adjectives

Name _____

smaller kite   smallest kite

Add **er** to an adjective when you compare two people, places or things.
smaller child   louder noise

Add **est** to an adjective when you compare three or more people, places or things.
smallest child   loudest noise

In the sentences below, circle the correct form of the adjective in the parentheses.

Example ➤ Gina was the (**older**, oldest) of the two girls.
1. Of the two towels, this one feels (**softer**, softest).
2. His story was the (longer, **longest**) one in his class.
3. Which of these two bananas is (**smaller**, smallest)?
4. The prices at Wong's store are the (lower, **lowest**) in town.
5. The kitchen is the (warmer, **warmest**) room in our house.
6. This cake is (**sweeter**, sweetest) than that pie.
7. Yesterday was the (colder, **coldest**) day we've had this winter.
8. Kenny is the (**taller**, tallest) of the twins.
9. My desk is the (**neater**, neatest) of the two.
10. Robin is the (smarter, **smartest**) of the children.
11. Let's watch the (shorter, **shortest**) movie on TV.
12. Which one of your parents is (**older**, oldest)?
13. Susan is the (**prettier**, prettiest) of the two girls.
14. The redwood is the (larger, **largest**) tree in the world.

Page 79

Page 80

Adjectives

Name _____

Spelling Rules

big   bigger   biggest

When an adjective ends in a single consonant following a single vowel, double the final consonant and add er or est.
bigger   biggest

When an adjective ends in a silent e, drop the final e and add er or est.
wider   widest

If a word ends in y, following a consonant, change the y to i and add er or est.
sillier   silliest

Copy each adjective below. Then write the two forms it uses in comparison. Follow the spelling rules above.

Example ➤ hot—   hot,   hotter,   hottest

1. easy—	easy	easier	easiest
2. brave—	brave	braver	bravest
3. scary—	scary	scarier	scariest
4. red—	red	redder	reddest
5. nice—	nice	nicer	nicest
6. hungry—	hungry	hungrier	hungriest
7. blue—	blue	bluer	bluest
8. noisy—	noisy	noisier	noisiest
9. flat—	flat	flatter	flattest
10. fast—	fast	faster	fastest

On another piece of paper, write a sentence showing comparison for each of the following adjectives.

safer, safest   richer, richest   tighter, tightest
happier, happiest   bluer, bluest   riper, ripest

Page 80

Answer Key

  Name _____

Adjectives
More and Most

more delicious   most delicious

Longer adjectives are usually compared by the use of **more** and **most**.

Use **more** to compare two people, places or things.
Dale is **more** helpful than Pat.

Use **most** to compare three or more people, places or things.
Holly was the **most** helpful student in the class.

If you use more or most, do not use er or est.
right: This tree is **larger** than that one.
wrong: This tree is **more larger** than that one.

In the sentences below, circle the correct form of the adjective in the parentheses.

Example > Jose seems (more happier, (happier)) than Juan.

1. This is the (more useful, (most useful)) book in the library.
2. Brand X keeps my clothes ((cleaner,) more cleaner) than Brand Y.
3. The movie was the (most scarlest, (scariest)) I've ever seen.
4. Donna is the ((more beautiful) most beautiful) of the twins.
5. Ricky is (more taller, (taller)) than his dad.
6. Of all the flavors, chocolate is the (more delicious, (most delicious))
7. Nicky's joke was ((funnier,) more funnier) than mine.
8. Eileen's report was the (most neatest, (neatest)) one in her class.
9. That rose is the (more unusual, (most unusual)) one I have.

Page 81

 Adjectives Name _____

good   2nd place   better   best

A few adjectives change to completely new words when they are used to compare things. Two of these adjectives are the words **good** and **bad**.

good—This is a good book.
better—My book is better than your book.
best—This is the best book I've ever read.
bad—The weather is bad today.
worse—The weather is worse today than yesterday.
worst—Today's weather is the worst of the winter.

In the sentences below, circle the correct form of the adjective in the parentheses.

Example > Lunch today is (good, (better,) best) than yesterday.

1. This is the (bad, worse, (worst)) pizza I have ever eaten.
2. My shoes are in (bad, (worse,) worst) condition than yours.
3. My grades are the (good, better, (best)) in the class.
4. Mother has a ((good,) better, best) set of dishes.
5. This tool is the (good, better, (best)) one I have.
6. I wore my (bad, worse, (worst)) jeans to the picnic.
7. My brownies are (good, (better,) best) than yours.
8. This is a ((bad,) worse, worst) snowstorm.
9. This one looks even (good, (better,) best) than that one.
10. My brother's room looks (bad, (worse,) worst) than mine.
11. Your tennis shoes have the (good, better, (best)) soles.
12. This headache is the (bad, worse, (worst)) I've ever had.

Page 82

Name _____

Nouns
Adjectives
Review

big, beautiful (rose)

In the sentences below, underline the adjectives and circle the nouns they describe. Do not use a or an.

Example > My (dog) is young and frisky.

1. Dad bought a new blue (car.)
2. This (winter) has been cold and icy.
3. The furry (cat) hid under my back (porch.)
4. The brave (firemen) rescued the small (children.)
5. My parents bought a new (table) and (lamp.)
6. Many (birds) ate from our large (birdhouse.)
7. The American (flag) is red, white and blue.
8. Jeff has one (brother) and two (sisters.)
9. I needed a sharp (knife) to cut the tough (meat.)
10. The handsome (man) married the beautiful (lady.)
11. The mysterious (spaceship) landed in the dense (forest.)
12. Ten chocolate (cupcakes) were on the large (plate.)
13. The longest (race) of the day lasted one (hour.)
14. Your tennis (shoes) look newer than mine.
15. The young (children) walked along the sandy (beach.)
16. Ten (clowns) climbed out of the tiny (car.)
17. My dog chased the little, black (kitten) up a tree.
18. Susan made six (bibs) for her tiny (nephew.)
19. Many (people) attended the big (race) last (Saturday.)
20. The funniest (act) had the two crazy (clowns.)

Page 83

Name _____

Adverbs

An adverb answers the questions, How?, When? or Where? about verbs. Many adverbs end in ly when answering the question, How?

Our team won the game easily.   How?

Circle the adverb in each sentence. In the book below, tell which question it answers.

Example > My birthday is (today.)

1. The children played (quietly) at home.
2. We went to the movie (yesterday.)
3. My friends are coming (inside) to play.
4. The child cut his meat (carefully.)
5. The girls went (upstairs) to get their coats.
6. The play-off games start (tomorrow.)
7. The boys walked (slowly) toward the bus.
8. The teacher said, "Write your name (neatly.)"
9. We ate (outside) on a picnic table.

Example > When	My Book of Adverbs	5. Where
1. How	How? When? Where?	6. When
2. When		7. How
3. Where		8. How
4. How		9. Where

Page 84

Answer Key

Page 85

Adverbs

Name _____

Adverbs modify verbs or adjectives and tell how, when or where.

How—I read slowly.
Where—I read inside.
When—I was reading today.

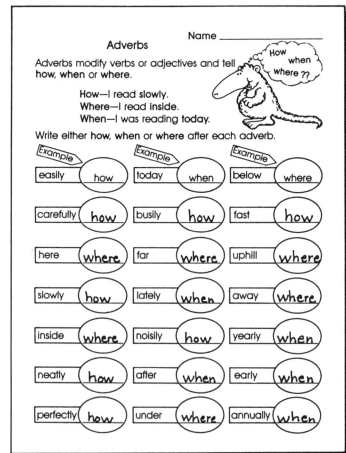

Write either how, when or where after each adverb.

Example	easily	how	Example	today	when	Example	below	where
	carefully	how		busily	how		fast	how
	here	where		far	where		uphill	where
	slowly	how		lately	when		away	where
	inside	where		noisily	how		yearly	when
	neatly	how		after	when		early	when
	perfectly	how		under	where		annually	when

Page 85

Page 86

Where?
The monkeys are inside.

Adverbs

Name _____

In the sentences below, write an adverb on the line to complete each sentence. The word in parentheses tells the kind of adverb to write. Do not use an adverb more than once. Answers will vary.

Example > The car is ___here___ .   (where)
1. Our team played _____ .   (when)
2. Brian writes _____ .   (how)
3. The cows move _____ .   (how)
4. Melissa will dance _____ .   (when)
5. My dog went _____ .   (where)
6. We ran _____ .   (how)
7. The choir sang _____ .   (how)
8. The cat purred _____ .   (where)
9. Hilary spoke _____ .   (how)
10. We'll go on our vacation _____ .   (when)
11. The sign goes _____ .   (where)
12. Mother brought the groceries _____ .   (where)
13. David read the directions _____ .   (how)
14. We'll be leaving _____ .   (when)
15. We have three bedrooms _____ .   (where)
16. Our family goes on a vacation _____ .   (when)
17. Jim ran _____ down the street.   (how)
18. They _____ laid the baby in the crib.   (how)
19. The man went _____ with his paper.   (where)
20. My dad gets a raise in pay _____ .   (when)

Page 86

Page 87

I can run faster.

Name _____

Verbs
Adverbs
Review

In the sentences below, draw a line under every adverb and circle every verb. Write the verbs and adverbs in the proper column after each sentence.

	Verb	Adverb
Example > We did our chores quietly.	did	quietly
1. Jason got his bicycle early.	got	early
2. Slowly, I cleaned my room.	cleaned	slowly
3. Lucy often rides her horse.	rides	often
4. We walked cautiously on the ice.	walked	cautiously
5. I washed my car today.	washed	today
6. Suddenly, it started to snow.	started	suddenly
7. Derek took his wagon outside.	took	outside
8. The child used the scissors carefully.	used	carefully
9. Jackie went home early.	went	early
10. Bill slid safely into second base.	slid	safely
11. Shari happily got 100% on her test.	got	happily
12. My cousin came again to visit.	came	again
13. Earlier, I helped the principal.	helped	Earlier
14. The soldiers bravely fought.	fought	bravely
15. We quickly finished the puzzle.	finished	quickly
16. Yesterday, I baked brownies.	baked	Yesterday
17. Susie takes her shower upstairs.	takes	upstairs
18. My dad gets his paycheck monthly.	gets	monthly
19. The twins threw the toys everywhere.	threw	everywhere
20. The mouse crept quietly out.	crept	quietly out

Page 87

Page 88

Nouns-Pronouns
Adjectives
Verbs-Adverbs
Review

Name _____

In the sentences below, label each of the following.

N—for noun   Adj —for adjective
P —for pronoun   Adv—for adverb
V—for verb

      Adj Adj N V   Adv
Example > The little girl ran outside.

  P   V   Adj   N   Adv
1. We feed the birds regularly.

  N   V   Adj Adj   N   Adv
2. Derek planted a maple tree yesterday.

  N   V   P   Adj N
3. Charles wrote them a letter.

  P   V Adj Adj   N
4. They have two small dogs.

  N   V   V   Adv
5. Rosie will be dancing tomorrow.

  Adj   N   V   Adv
6. The toys were everywhere.

  Adj Adj   N   V   V   Adv
7. The three children are going swimming today.

  P   V   V Adv
8. You can eat now.

  P   V   Adj N   Adv
9. They washed the car carefully.

  Adj Adj   N   V Adj   N
10. Several thirsty children drank cold lemonade.

  P   V Adj   N   Adv
11. We run three miles often.

  Adj   N   V   V   Adv
12. The chorus has been singing beautifully.

  P   V   N Adj   N
13. He gave Chuck five dollars.

  N   V Adj   N   Adv
14. Pam washed the dishes slowly.

  Adj Adj   N   V   Adv
15. That tiny baby was sleeping soundly.

Page 88

Answer Key

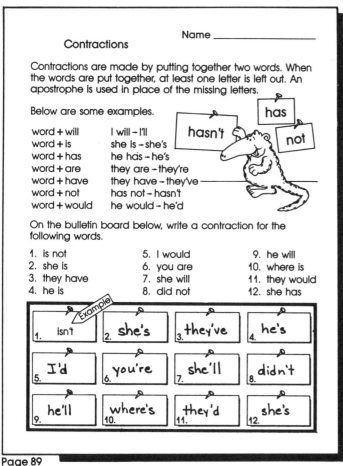

Name _____

Contractions

Contractions are made by putting together two words. When the words are put together, at least one letter is left out. An apostrophe is used in place of the missing letters.

Below are some examples.

word + will	I will – I'll
word + is	she is – she's
word + has	he has – he's
word + are	they are – they're
word + have	they have – they've
word + not	has not – hasn't
word + would	he would – he'd

On the bulletin board below, write a contraction for the following words.

1. is not
2. she is
3. they have
4. he is
5. I would
6. you are
7. she will
8. did not
9. he will
10. where is
11. they would
12. she has

1. isn't (Example)	2. she's	3. they've	4. he's
5. I'd	6. you're	7. she'll	8. didn't
9. he'll	10. where's	11. they'd	12. she's

Page 89

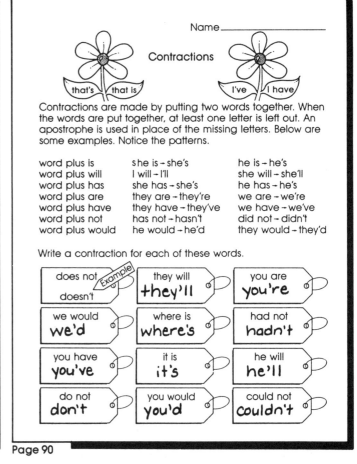

Name _____

Contractions

that's / that is   I've / I have

Contractions are made by putting two words together. When the words are put together, at least one letter is left out. An apostrophe is used in place of the missing letters. Below are some examples. Notice the patterns.

word plus is	she is – she's	he is – he's
word plus will	I will – I'll	she will – she'll
word plus has	she has – she's	he has – he's
word plus are	they are – they're	we are – we're
word plus have	they have – they've	we have – we've
word plus not	has not – hasn't	did not – didn't
word plus would	he would – he'd	they would – they'd

Write a contraction for each of these words.

does not — doesn't (Example)	they will — they'll	you are — you're
we would — we'd	where is — where's	had not — hadn't
you have — you've	it is — it's	he will — he'll
do not — don't	you would — you'd	could not — couldn't

Page 90

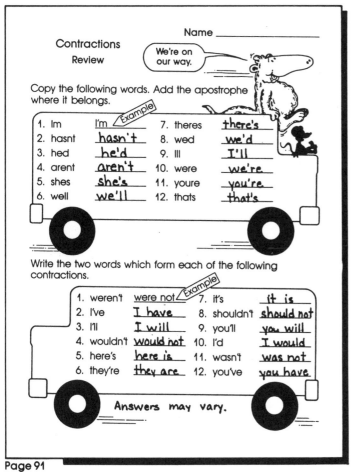

Name _____

Contractions Review

We're on our way.

Copy the following words. Add the apostrophe where it belongs.

1. Im — I'm (Example)
2. hasnt — hasn't
3. hed — he'd
4. arent — aren't
5. shes — she's
6. well — we'll
7. theres — there's
8. wed — we'd
9. Ill — I'll
10. were — we're
11. youre — you're
12. thats — that's

Write the two words which form each of the following contractions.

1. weren't — were not (Example)
2. I've — I have
3. I'll — I will
4. wouldn't — would not
5. here's — here is
6. they're — they are
7. it's — it is
8. shouldn't — should not
9. you'll — you will
10. I'd — I would
11. wasn't — was not
12. you've — you have

Answers may vary.

Page 91

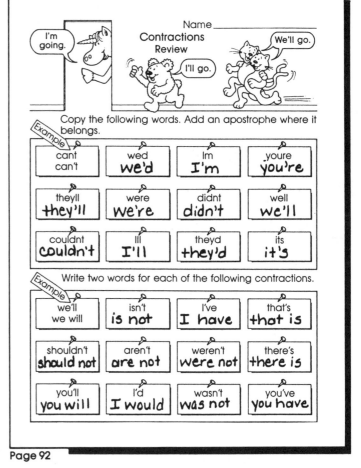

Name _____

Contractions Review

I'm going.   I'll go.   We'll go.

Copy the following words. Add an apostrophe where it belongs.

cant — can't (Example)	wed — we'd	Im — I'm	youre — you're
theyll — they'll	were — we're	didnt — didn't	well — we'll
couldnt — couldn't	Ill — I'll	theyd — they'd	its — it's

Write two words for each of the following contractions.

we'll — we will (Example)	isn't — is not	I've — I have	that's — that is
shouldn't — should not	aren't — are not	weren't — were not	there's — there is
you'll — you will	I'd — I would	wasn't — was not	you've — you have

Page 92

Answer Key

Page 93

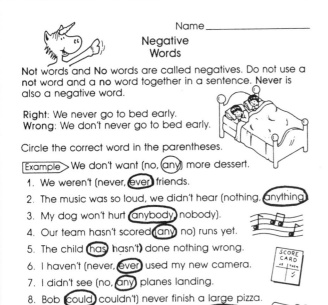

Name _____

Negative Words

Not words and No words are called negatives. Do not use a not word and a no word together in a sentence. Never is also a negative word.

Right: We never go to bed early.
Wrong: We don't never go to bed early.

Circle the correct word in the parentheses.

Example > We don't want (no, **any**) more dessert.

1. We weren't (never, **ever**) friends.
2. The music was so loud, we didn't hear (nothing, **anything**).
3. My dog won't hurt (**anybody**, nobody).
4. Our team hasn't scored (**any**, no) runs yet.
5. The child (**has**, hasn't) done nothing wrong.
6. I haven't (never, **ever**) used my new camera.
7. I didn't see (no, **any**) planes landing.
8. Bob (**could**, couldn't) never finish a large pizza.
9. My cousin hasn't gone (nowhere, **anywhere**).
10. You (**should**, shouldn't) never slam the door.
11. Connie, (**are**, aren't) you never going to finish this?
12. I (haven't, **have**) never been to England.
13. Judy (**is**, isn't) never on time for school.
14. There (**was**, wasn't) never enough snow to ski.
15. Steve didn't (never, **ever**) forget his mother's birthday.

Page 94

Negative Words

Name _____

The words not, no and **never** are negative words. You must avoid using two negative words in a sentence.

Right—There is no popcorn left.
Wrong—There isn't no popcorn left.

Circle the correct word in the parentheses.

Example > Michelle (**could** couldn't) run no faster.

1. I didn' (**ever** never) wear braces.
2. My teacher hasn't (none, **any**) of our grades yet.
3. Kim couldn't drive (no one, **anyone**) home.
4. Isn't (**anybody** nobody) going with me?
5. My family (hasn't, **has**) no time to travel this year.
6. I don't like to go (nowhere, **anywhere**) alone.
7. Chris (**has** hasn't) done no homework.
8. We (wouldn't, **would**) never lie to you.
9. Why didn't I get (none **any**)?
10. Andy hasn't (no, **any**) film for his camera.
11. Diana, (**are** aren't) you never going to finish this?
12. Todd (wasn't, **was**) saving no money at all.
13. We aren't able to do (**any** no) magic tricks.
14. Won't you (never, **ever**) return my record?

Write a sentence for each of the following words: never, nothing, don't, nobody.

_____
_____
_____
_____

Page 95

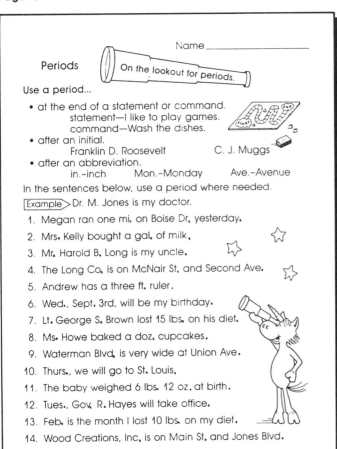

Name _____

Periods

On the lookout for periods.

Use a period...

- at the end of a statement or command.
  statement—I like to play games.
  command—Wash the dishes.
- after an initial.
  Franklin D. Roosevelt   C. J. Muggs
- after an abbreviation.
  in.-inch   Mon.-Monday   Ave.-Avenue

In the sentences below, use a period where needed.

Example > Dr. M. Jones is my doctor.

1. Megan ran one mi. on Boise Dr. yesterday.
2. Mrs. Kelly bought a gal. of milk.
3. Mr. Harold B. Long is my uncle.
4. The Long Co. is on McNair St. and Second Ave.
5. Andrew has a three ft. ruler.
6. Wed., Sept. 3rd, will be my birthday.
7. Lt. George S. Brown lost 15 lbs. on his diet.
8. Ms. Howe baked a doz. cupcakes.
9. Waterman Blvd. is very wide at Union Ave.
10. Thurs., we will go to St. Louis.
11. The baby weighed 6 lbs. 12 oz. at birth.
12. Tues., Gov. R. Hayes will take office.
13. Feb. is the month I lost 10 lbs. on my diet.
14. Wood Creations, Inc. is on Main St. and Jones Blvd.

Page 96

Name _____

Commas

Entering Atlanta, Georgia

Use a comma...

- between the day and the year in a date.
  November 17, 1955
- between a city and a state.
  Denver, Colorado
- in a series of three or more persons or things.
  apples, oranges and plums.*

In the sentences below, place commas where needed.

Example > Matthew was born August 7, 1978.

1. Kara, Sue and Patti played together.
2. On May 12, 1980, we moved to Dallas, Texas.
3. The Statue of Liberty is in New York City, New York.
4. Grandma and Grandpa were married June 12, 1942.
5. Mia has roses, pansies and daisies in her garden.
6. The American flag is red, white and blue.
7. I moved from Miami, Florida to Cleveland, Ohio.
8. Hawaii became a state August 21, 1959.
9. Tommy, Gary, Adam and Jerry are my best friends.
10. On Monday, Tuesday and Wednesday it snowed.
11. John F. Kennedy was shot November 22, 1963.
12. We drive through Chicago, Illinois on our way to Madison, Wisconsin.

*Some textbooks place a comma before the and.
apples, oranges, and plums

Answer Key

Page 97

Name _____

Commas

Use a comma...

- after the greeting and closing in a friendly letter.
  Dear Nina,   Yours truly, Jason

- to set off a direct quotation from the rest of the sentence.
  Andy said, "Meet me at 7:00."

- after yes or no at the beginning of a sentence or after the name of a person spoken to.
  Yes, I'm feeling better.   Amy, how do you feel?

In the sentences below, use a comma where needed.

Example▷ Terry, what is your dog's name?

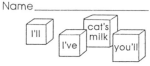

1. Christine asked, "How old are you?"
2. Mother said, "I'm going to work."
3. Yes, I have finished the dishes.
4. Nicky, what T.V. program are you watching?
5. No, I have not finished my homework.
6. Lorna, where did you go on your vacation?

In the letter below, use commas where needed.

> Dear Rachel,
>
> Did you go to Seattle, Washington last summer? I went to visit my cousins in Detroit, Michigan. When I got home Mom said, "Debbie did you have fun?"
>
> I said, "Yes, it was great."
>
> Rachel, I hope to see you soon.
>
> Your friend,
>
> Debbie

Page 97

Page 98

Name _____

Commas

A comma is used...

- to separate the day of the month from the year.   May 3, 1976
- to separate a city from a state or country.   Dallas, Texas
- to set off the name of a person spoken to.   Brad, come here.
- after yes or no at the beginning of a sentence.
  Yes, I can come.
- to set words apart in a series.* I like apples, grapes and pears,
- after the first complete thought in a sentence with two thoughts.   Hurry up, or we'll be late.
- after the greeting of a friendly letter and after the closing of every letter.   Dear Anita,   Sincerely, Dan
- to set off a direct quotation.   "I'm coming," said Al.

In the following sentences, use commas where they are needed.

Example▷ Teddy, did you go to Utah, Nevada and Colorado?

1. My parents were married March 24, 1967.
2. After swimming, skating is my favorite sport.
3. I signed my letter Yours truly, Tracy.
4. "Patti, I'll be home late," said mother.
5. On December 6, 1981, Carlos came to America.
6. Exams will be Tuesday, Wednesday and Thursday.
7. Sarah missed the bus, so she had to walk home.
8. I took my notebook to class, but I forgot my pencil.
9. Tim asked, "Is that a good book?"
10. On the way home, I ran into a fence.
11. Yes, I bought cereal, milk, bread and tuna.
12. We went from Miami, Florida to Tulsa, Oklahoma.

*Some textbooks teach that a comma is required before the "and".

Page 98

Page 99

Name _____

Apostrophes

Use an apostrophe...

- in possessive nouns.
  singular–Teddy's record   Sharon's game
  plural–men's club   bears' tracks

- in contractions.
  I am–I'm   did not–didn't

In the groups of words below, make the underlined word show possession by using an apostrophe.

Example▷ <u>Kevins</u> baseball.   Kevin's

1. the <u>firemens</u> boots   1. firemen's
2. three <u>trains</u> tracks   2. trains'
3. a <u>ships</u> decks   3. ship's
4. <u>Lynns</u> house   4. Lynn's
5. several <u>friends</u> games   5. friends'
6. many <u>players</u> uniforms   6. players'

Write the contraction of these words by using an apostrophe.

Example▷ could not <u>couldn't</u>

1. he will _he'll_   5. were not _weren't_
2. you are _you're_   6. we have _we've_
3. he is _he's_   7. they are _they're_
4. it is _It's_   8. she will _she'll_

Page 99

Page 100

Name _____

Quotation Marks

Have you read, "Where the River Begins"?

Use quotation marks...

- to set off a direct quotation.
  The teacher said, "Kate, you got 100% on your test."

- around titles of poems, stories and reports.
  Todd read, "The Owl and The Pussycat."

Quotation marks are placed after the period or question mark.

In the sentences below, place quotation marks where needed.

Example▷ "Turn off the lights," Mother said.

1. Mr. Gordon asked, "Daniel, are you going with me?"
2. Grandma read me the story, "The Rat in the Hat."
3. "Miracle on 34th Street" is one of my favorite movies.
4. "Are you going to the play?" Millie asked.
5. Anna gave a report called, "Indians of the Southwest."
6. My brother can read, "Spot Goes to School."
7. Luke remarked, "It's very cold today."
8. Gavin read a report titled, "Inside the Personal Computer."
9. "Let's get together tomorrow," said Diana.
10. Have you read the poem called, "Dancers Delight?"
11. Joey said, "Dave, let's play after school."
12. Jenny's report was titled, "Great Painters."

Page 100

Answer Key

Name _____

Quotation Marks
Apostrophes

Use quotation marks...

• before and after the words of every direct quotation.
  Margie asked, "What's for lunch?"

• around titles of stories, song titles, poems and reports.
  I read the poem, "Rip Van Winkle."

Use an apostrophe...

• to show where letters have been left out of contractions.
  they'll   we're   wouldn't

• to show ownership or possession.
  Donna's shoes   hikers' boots

In the following sentences, use quotation marks and apostrophes where they are needed.

Example > Wasn't "The Rose and the Key" a good story?

1. The players' equipment was kept in their lockers.
2. I've finished my report, "Famous Athletes."
3. Jennifer replied, "I'd love to come to your party."
4. My poem, "The Beautiful Butterfly," won first prize.
5. Robbie's hamsters are frisky.
6. It's Ginny's coat that Sandy is wearing.
7. Aren't the boys' bikes in the garage?
8. We're doing our report on rockets together.
9. The reporters' stories were all too long.
10. My friend's birthday is tomorrow.
11. "How to Handle Snakes," was the title of my report.
12. My sister's favorite album is Michael Jackson's "Thriller."

Page 101

Name _____

Punctuation Marks   Review

In the sentences below, place periods, commas, apostrophes and quotation marks where needed.

Example > "Yes, I'm going to the movie," said Ian.

1. Our family lives in Memphis, Tennessee.
2. The boys' bicycles were new.
3. I've an uncle named T. R. Mayberry.
4. Mrs. Jordan, Lori and Bonnie went to the fair.
5. Aunt Helen said, "I'll be home late tonight."
6. Didn't you measure 5 ft. last year?
7. Willy asked, "How much is the candy?"
8. Mother read us, "The Very Busy Spider."
9. I'm going to buy books, erasers and pencils.
10. Gail, were you born Dec. 14, 1975?
11. They're reading, "The Ships' Voyage,"
12. Sandy, please buy a lb. of apples.
13. Holly said, "Mom and Dad were married May 2, 1955."
14. Shouldn't we read, "Travel the U S A?"
15. We're going to Dr. Gibbon's office.
16. The three boys' sweaters were left in Reid, Ohio.
17. "Ebb Tide" is Joseph's favorite old song.
18. Mr. Evans, were you in Dallas, Texas, on May 1, 1985?
19. Who's going to read the main character's part?
20. Vince asked, "Where's the car's lights?"

Page 102

About the book . . .

This book offers a wide variety of activities that provide a knowledge of the "rules and regulations" of proper English usage. Some of the basic skills addressed are: ABC order, parts of speech, plurals, verb tense, punctuation, sentences, possession, etc.
Illustrated to enhance student motivation, these activities are packed with skill drills.

About the author . . .

Jean Agatstein is a practicing teacher whose innate ability to understand the needs of both teachers and students is evident in her writing. This ability has been developed during more than twenty years of teaching at all levels of the elementary curriculum.

Author: Jean Agatstein
Editor: Lee Quackenbush
Artists: Jim Price/Carol Tiernon
Cover Art: Jan Vonk